Poetical Works of Richard Watson

With a Brief Sketch of the Author

———

From Nature's self my Muse doth spring, —
Though roughly clad, to her I'll cling;
And where the Tees rolls meandering
The woods among,
I'll tune my mountain lyre, and sing
My rustic song.

Richard Watson.

PANTIANOS
CLASSICS

Published by Pantianos Classics

ISBN-13: 978-1-78987-478-5

First published in 1884

Contents

Preface

More than twenty years have expired since Richard Watson published his now very scarce and, by the old standards of Teesdale, greatly-treasured little book.

Since that period his "Mountain Lyre" has been by no means mute. The character — the scenery — the traditionary lore — blended with the hopes and fears, the joys and sorrows of his fellow dalesmen — having been woven into his songs and rhymes, have made his name familiar as a "household word" throughout his native dale.

Of late there has been a steadily growing demand for the publication of his writings, which have been delayed for some considerable time, — more, perhaps, through the misfortune than the fault of the author, — and is only now accelerated by the kindness and public spirit of the gentleman to whom they are dedicated and others, chief of whom is the cultured and genial proprietor of the *Teesdale Mercury*, whose columns, ever open to the poet, have done so much to extend his fame.

The assistance rendered to civilization by poetry has had ample recognition. Poets having long been among the acknowledged teachers of mankind.

In the whirl and tumult of our present day feverish race for wealth and honours, or among the masses the fierce strife for existence, how essential is the simple freshness of the poet's teachings for the prevention of our ideas of refinement and true culture being scorched from the soul.

There will be many take up this book who may not be acquainted with the vernacular of Teesdale, in which a good many of the pieces are written, or whose interest may not be quickened by an acquaintance with the characters or locality described. We would ask them not to judge Mr. Watson's songs or poetry as they would the songs of a Beranger, a Bums or a Moore, or the poetry of a Byron or a Shelley.

The author is essentially a working man poet, and though it is largely the experiences and thoughts of that class which colour the production of his Muse, yet his "education" has made him quite familiar with those wondrous spirits with which poets of all time have so wondrously conjured, "That indestructible love of flowers and odours, dews and clear waters, soft airs and sounds, bright skies, woodland solitudes, and moonlight bowers, which are the material elements of poetry."

J. M.

Preface to First Edition

In bringing these Poems before the public, I beg to remind my readers that I have not had a classical education; therefore they must not expect to meet with that elegance and refinement which have graced the writings of other poets of our isle, who have won for themselves laurels which will never wither. I may truly say, with Burns, —

> "I am nae poet, in a sense,
>   But just a rhymer, like, by chance,
>   And hae to learning nae pretence;
>   Yet, what the matter?
>   Whene'er my Muse does on me glance,
>   I jingle at her."

Though the greater part of my readers may be better accustomed to the polished songs of the valley, yet they may not be indifferent to the wild strains of the mountain. The majority of the Poems contained in this little book have been composed at the mine-shop, — on the moor between Middleton and Stanhope, — at night, after the toils of the day. At the request of my friends I have published them. I would have published a larger number, but I thought it was better to look ere I leaped. I will publish another number shortly, should this one meet with the approbation of the public. Meanwhile, I return my sincere thanks to my subscribers for their kind encouragement.

Richard Watson.

Middleton-in-Teesdale,
  March, 1862.

Brief Sketch of the Author

Richard Watson is the son of the late William Watson, who was a miner in the employment of the London Lead Company. He was born March 16th, 1833, at Middleton-in-Teesdale. At the age of six he was sent to the Company's school, — erected at that place for the education of their workmen's children, — where, under the tuition of Mr. John Hyslop, the schoolmaster, he received a tolerable education.

His father, who was then struggling to maintain a large family, could not afford to let him remain long at school, so at the age of ten he went to labour at the mines, where he has been ever since. The father, whose powers had been exerted to the utmost to procure food for his family, began to fail in strength, and at the age of forty-seven departed this life, leaving the subject of this memoir, at the age of fourteen, with a widowed mother, two brothers, and six sisters, to battle in the midst of poverty with the cares and anxieties of this cold selfish world. His talent for poetry was shown at an early age. While at school, he often amused his playmates with extempore pieces of rhyme, and often did he delight his fellow labourers at the mine with his witty effusions.

But it seems his poetry at that time was composed simply for his own amusement, as it was suffered to be forgot, he not committing it to writing. The first poem he printed was the Dialogue between the Tower and Bridge, which was published in the *Teesdale Mercury*, and it is to the worthy editor of that paper the author owes much of his fame and popularity. The poem was received enthusiastically by the public. Since then various poems of his have appeared in print.

His style is more like that of Burns than of any of the other poets, and, indeed, an air of drollery very similar to that manifested by the great poet of rustic life pervades his poems, and shows talent and originality which prove him to be a poet of no mean order. May he still go on, and tell the tales and sing of the scenes of our native dale! And cold is the heart of the man who, having the means, will not encourage the efforts of rising genius in a son of toil.

"Dante."

Baliol's Tower and the Railway Bridge

A DIALOGUE

"All else was hush'd as Nature's closed e'e;
The silent moon shone high o'er tower and tree:
The chilly frost beneath the silver beam,
Crept, gently-crusting o'er the glittering stream."

— Burns.

RECITATIVE

The sun had set behind the hill,
And Nature was all hush'd and still,
Except the night's cold sighing breeze,
And peaceful murmur of the Tees.
Upon the river's brink I stood:
I view'd the sparkling rippling flood.
Which seemed one mass of diamonds bright.
Illumined by the moon's pale light.
I could discern, between the trees.
The Railway Bridge which spans the Tees;
And near me, on the rocky height.
Old Barnard's Tower appear'd in sight,
With the crumbling ivied walls,
Which once form'd spacious rooms and halls;
But all are gone, except the cell
Wherein the hermit Frank did dwell.
And, while I view'd such scenes combined,
A train of thoughts rose in my mind:
I thought upon the days gone by,
The warlike days of chivalry,
When Scotch and English warriors rude
Met on these banks in deadly feud;
But from my dreamy thoughts I woke,
A thundering voice the silence broke.
With startled gaze I looked around
To see whence came that threatening sound:
Twas from the Tower I soon did prove,
Directed to the Bridge above.
With voice beyond the power of man.
In words like these it thus began: —

TOWER

Vile Bridge! how high you rear your head
Above the river's rocky bed;
You'll think yourself a noble structure,
A famous piece of architecture;
No doubt you'll be puffed up with pride
When fiery engines o'er you glide,
While Nature's beauty you deface;
Built by a sordid, plebian race,
Whose deeds, compared with those of old,
Ought not in history to be told.
Alas! it makes me sorely weep:
It makes my whole foundation creep
To see tall trees and meadows fine
Destroyed to make a railway line,
Where once the oak's proud branches spread,
And where the antler'd deer were fed.
Oh! for the time when in the morn
I heard the merry bugle horn:
When Deepdale woods echo'd the sound
Of huntsman's voice and crying hound:
When England's monarch, with his train
Of Teesdale's loyal valiant men,
Well tried their coursers' highest skill.
And swiftly sped o'er dale and hill;
O'er meadow, brake, and streamlet clear.
Pursued till eve the bounding deer;
And when night darkened Nature's face,
And stopp'd the hot and eager chase.
Within my walls they met around
The groaning board, with dainties crown'd;
And minstrels sung their lays divine.
While heroes quaff'd the sparkling wine.
But, ah! those joys are fled away,
Those' faces bright are gone to clay,
And others have sprung up instead,
Who are by modern fancies led.
I hate! I hate those modern ways;
Give back to me the good old days.

RECITATIVE

It ceas'd. The Bridge began to speak,

9

And every massive beam did creak;
While borne upon the nightly breeze,
These words were wafted down the Tees: —

BRIDGE

Old doating ruin! be at rest,
Thou emblem of dark ages past,
And relic of the feudal times, —
Days of oppression and of crimes —
When haughty nobles, in that day,
O'er abject serfdom held the sway:
When want and woe went hand in hand.
And civil broils disturbed the land.
Though some might drink their wine, and glide
With reckless glee down pleasure's tide,
Or with the sword might gain renown,
Yet freedom's cause was trampl'd down;
But freedom's sun doth now arise,
From whose bright light oppression flies.
As morning vapour flies away
Before the golden orb of day;
And men now prize the arts of peace.
While trade and commerce do increase.
And railway lines are now laid down,
Extending trade from town to town.
And binding men more closely still.
In friendship, union, and goodwill;
And peace and wealth our land doth crown,
While, castle walls are mouldering down.

TOWER

You're speaking loud, but rather fast;
Let modems look back to the past,
And see how their forefathers stood
On battle-fields dyed red with blood,
And valiantly withstood their foes,
For freedom, and for England's cause,
When many a plundering Scottish band
With fire and sword raged through the land.
Moss-troopers, arm'd with sword and spear,
Keeping the country side in fear,
Like rav'nous wolves in search of prey,

10

They drove the flocks and herds away;
Oft have our warriors sallied forth,
To check those plunderers of the north,
And make them quickly to recede
Back o'er the borders, o'er the Tweed,
Teaching them to look around.
And know they were on English ground.
Thus did they fight, and felt no fear
Of Spanish Don, or French Monsieur,
And England stood with honour crown'd.
And fear'd by all the nations round.
Yet moderns scarcely cast a thought
On the great deeds their fathers wrought.
Nor ever think their father's merit
Procured the freedom they inherit.
Though time's rough hand on me is seen,
I'm but a wreck of what I've been.
But leave me not one hoary wall
Than live to see old England fall!

BRIDGE

Old England fall! It cannot be;
That's what we'll neither of us see,
For crown'd with wealth she now stands forth
The greatest nation on the earth;
Her hardy sons are brave and free,
Her banner waves o'er every sea,
And treasures to her feet are brought
From countries of the earth remote.
No more the Scots molest our land,
Nor meet our warriors hand to hand;
We count them now no longer foes, —
The thistle's twined with the rose!
In peace we now united are,
Unbroken by the din of war.
Then hold thy peace, thou braggart old.
And leave thy youthful crimes untold;
Speak not to me of days of yore.
Thy power is gone for evermore!

RECITATIVE

Their speaking ceas'd. I left the spot,
    And took my homeward way;

11

But whether they'll be friends or not
    Is more than I can say.

Thoughts

Suggested on viewing a Stone near Wemmergill, Lunedale, Commonly Called "Robin Hood's Pennystone."

"And this our life, exempt from public haunt,
Finds tongues in trees, books in the running brooks,
Sermons in stones, and good in everything."

                                     — Shakespeare.

Say, curious stone, what brought thee here?
Why thou dost on this place appear,
    I fain would know.
And how thy base doth keep thee up.
When thou'rt so very wide at top.
    And strait below?

Say, was it some volcanic shock
That tore thee from thy native rock
    And parent sill —
And sent thee here, with thundering might.
Until at length thou did'st alight
    On this bleak hill?

Or was it when, with awful sweep,
The waters of the mighty deep
    Spread all around.
And rolling with the foaming tide.
Which left thee when it did subside
    Upon this ground?

Who knows but that, in ancient days,
Where thou dost stand was once a place
    Of sacred note;
Thou for an altar might suffice.
Where Druids, for the sacrifice,
    Their victims brought!

Had use of speech been given thee.
What strange things thou could'st tell to me
    Of ages past!

But words from thee I list in vain.
So as I am, I must remain,
     In mystery lost.
But let me thanks to heaven give.
That I in happier times do live,
     When Gospel light
In splendour casts its glorious rays,
And heathen darkness from its blaze.
     Hath taken flight

While light and knowledge round me spread.
Let me in wisdom's pathway tread,
     So that I may
At the right hand of God be found,
When thou with all the earth around
     Shall melt away!

The Quack Doctor

A Dialogue on a Pay Day

"And then o' doctor's saws and whittles
Of a' dimensions, shapes and mettles;
A' kinds o' boxes, mugs, and bottles;
                    He's sure to ha'e:
Their Latin names as fast he rattles
                    As A, B, C."

— Burns.

Matt. How is ta? Thou's a stranger, Bill.
Bill. Aw's fresh! an hope thou's sae thysel;
Here is my box, thi' pipe come fill,
     And sit ta down
An rist ti' legs. Az war'nt' tha will
     Hae been at town?

Matt. Wy, man! I went to draw my pay.
An aw hae been amused to-day, —
Disgusted, tu, as aw ma' say,
     Wi' a Quack Doctor,
Et aw left, when aw com away.
     On wid ez lecture.

13

He said he had some med'cine plann'd,
Et wad cure aught he took in hand;
A g'yapen crowd did round him stand
    Cocking their lugs,
Kiddy to swelly ez nonsense and
    Ez filthy drugs.

An then to prove ez statement true,
An show he t'human system knew,
He'd diagrams exposed to view,
    Et queerest forms;
Boxes o' pills, an bottles tu
    Fill'd wi' lang worms.

Bill. It's t'brass sec men are efter, Matt,
They knaw reet weel whar t'money's at;
To fleece fond folk, and sell thir ket.
    Is all thir trade;
Aw stopt thi' t'yal, — come tell ma what
    T'aud rascal said.

Matt. Wy, man, he then began to state,
How t'bluid frae t'heart did circilate,
An Marcury, how t'wad operate
    On t'human frame;
He said et bowels et wad inflate,
    An t'narves inflame.

"Ye come," he said, "o' doctor's wills,
An swelly up their mineral pills;
An then they mak ye up lang bills
    Beyond all sense;
While aw'll cure ye o' all yer ills
    For eighteen-pence."

To cure t'piles he said he'd power,
An convulsions ev half an hour.
An cleanse t'bluid when it was impure;
    Likewise engage
Consumptions an fevers to cure,
    Ev thir last stage.

Fistulas, fits, an inflammations,
Lumbago, scurvy, palpitations.

14

Gravel, scrofula, ulcerations.
   Coughs, colics, spasms,
Gout, swelled legs, excoriations.
   An rheumatisms.
Tic-doloreux, dimness o' t'seet,
Debility, cancers, corns o' t'feet,
Worms, cholera, tuthwark, gleet.
   An pains o' t'chist;
An other things he did repeat,
   Et haw hae mist.

He said to folk he had been saught,
Et had to t'brink o't' gr'yav been braught;
An his black drops an pills had wraught
   A perfect cure.
When t'doctors all round had thaught
   All hope was ow're.

An man! to see em mak good wage,
Frae folk o' this enleetn'd age.
It really put me ev a rage.
   To tell tha truth;
Aw could hae knock'd em reet of t'stage,
   An stopp'd ez mouth.

Bill. Sec men can talk t'h'yal length o' t'day,
They speak ev sec an oilen way,
Sae glib o' tongue, an what they say
   Appears sae plain,
Et folk are apt to think et they
   Are clever men.

O' t'docter's craft what hae they seen
Et they can cure folk sae cleen?
Like thou an me they will be green,
   Ev sec like matters;
Doctors et hez to t'college been,
   Ell be thir betters.

It stands wi' re'sen, if they'd power
Just half o't illnesses to cure.
They needn't travel t'country ower;
   They could sit down,
Wi' practice plenty, aw's weel sure,
   Ev ony town.

Thir tricks yan hardly can describe;
At better men they jeer and gibe;
They're just a mean, imposing tribe.
   Aw'll tell tha what,
Thar isn't yan et sud prescribe
   For our aud cat.

Matt. They're heartless rogues, thar is nae doubt;
Joe Brown, when he was poorly, saught
Yan o' thur quacks et gangs about,
   An the base villain
Near kill'd poor Joe, an fleec'd em out
   O' thirty shilling.

Bill. It's reet folk for thir folly pay;
Thar's some folk easy led astray,
Sae daft an ignorant are they,
   An sune deceived.
Nae matter what a knave may say
   He is believ'd.

Aw'd rather be ivver sae poor,
An hunger's sharpest pangs endure,
Without a farden to procure
   Claes to my back,
An beg about frae doure to doure.
   Than be a quack.

Matt. Sec men for ony crimes are fit,
Et do by fraud thir 'lieven's git;
But, Bill, I can nae longer sit,
   Aw mun away,
Aw hae three miles to travel yit,
   An' sae good day.

The Poor Box Robbery

A DIALOGUE

Jack. Good morning. Bob, is tha quite weel?
Bob. Aw's varra fresh, man; how's thysel?
Jack. Come, git ti pipe, an' sit down here.
An' tell ma what thou's gitten queer.

16

Bob. Aw hennut mickle fresh ta tell.
But aw'l sit down, an rist mysel,
For aw's just gannen off ta wark,
An' winnot be at yam till dark;
But hes tha hear't about t'poor box,
How t'rogue's g'yan an' brocken t'locks?
It's stannen just ahint t'church dour,
To collect money to gie t'poor.

Jack. Aw nivver hear't on't afore,
It's quite eneugh ta mak yan glore.
Ta mak awd t'yals folk's always plannen,
Aji' that's just like all t'rist ets gannen;
They git up t'yals to mak a laugh, —
But awd burds isn't catch'd wi' caff;
For't bein true, aw gritly doubt it, —
But pra'tha tell nia all alwut it.

Bob. Wy, it's as true as it can be.
Them et's menden t'church telt me;
For't bein' true there is na doubt,
T'police is tryin' to find it out.

Jack. Wy, pra'tha, man, when hes't been?
Aw thought folk had'nt been sae mean;
Aw thought sec folk we had'nt had;
Aw thought our town was not sae bad.

Bob. Wy, wy, but there's folks gawn about
For their awn ends will stick at nout;
They'll talk sae nicely and deceive.
An' run about and rob and thieve;
But, then, to gan et dyd at neet.
Or else et momen 'fore 'twas leet,
An' gan in t'church, an paze off t'locks,
An' gan wid money out et box;
At sec an hour, at sec a pl'yas
Tuv our town's a grit disgr'yas.

Jack. Aw dursent a g'yan for fifty pund,
An' travell't ower t'buryin-grund;
Aw dursent a g'yan and shown me f'yas
E' sec a dauly dismal pl'yas,
For fear some spirit aw sud meet,
Or boggle, that gans round et neet;
Or skeletons, wie rattlin' b'yans.
An' hear their awful, dismal gr'yans;
An' maybe, tu, yan cannot tell.
But yan mud meet awd Satan's sel'!

17

Wi' varry fear 'twad mak ma drop,
'Twad mak ma varry hair stand up!
For if aw'd been a thievish man,
It wad ha' been t'last pl'yas to gan.

Bob. Wy, as for boggles, an' sec as that.
Aw wad care nae mair nor my awd hat;
Aw cannot think et ghost or warth
'El ivver travel this awd y earth;
When they war here they had their share,
Like thou an' me, o' toil an' care;
An' them ets g'yan tu t'better land.
To come back here el nut demand;
An' them at's g'yan tu t'brumstane pit,
'El hae to suffer where they're at, —
There's n'yan to notish their request,
And gatan there el haud them fast.
When men hae pass'd ower Jordan's river,
They're dune with this awd yearth for ivver.

Jack. Aw've hear't about Dick Turpin bauld,
How he my'ad folk lug out their gauld;
But Dick wad nivver g'yan, aw shure,
An' stepp'd ower t'dyd to steal fra t'poor.
Wheivver's dune sae mean a theft,
If they hev ony conscience left,
Aw wish it may now smite them sore.
And bum them like a red-het pore!

Bob. Wy, thar'll be times, aw dunnot doubt it.
When they'll be troubled sare about it;
An' when their sperits are depress'd,
They'll think et honesty's the best.
But t'winnot answer, sittin' here.
For aw mun to my wark now steer;
We'll meet some other time an' crack,
Sae aw'll bid tha a good morning, Jack.

Brighter Days to Come!

"Hope springs eternal in the human breast:
Man never is, but always to be bless'd.
The soul, uneasy and conflned from home,
Rests and expatiates on a life to come."

— Pope.

While toss'd in life's rude fragile bark,
   'Mid foaming billows dashing round;
When all before seems drear and dark.
   And scarce a gleam of light is found;
Yet hope springs up amid the gloom,
Foretelling brighter days to come!

What though through life our way we grope,
   Weary, oppressed with grief and care.
It cheers the drooping heart to hope.
   It is unmanly to despair;
A blighted tree again may bloom,
And brighter, happier days may come!

Of what use is it to complain.
   Though this life's comforts be denied?
More satisfaction we will gain
   By looking on the brighter side;
Why murmur at our earthly doom?
Look forward, brighter days will come!

Think not our hopes and prospects all
   In dark oblivion will end.
In happier climes shall live that soul
   That does to mercy's voice attend;
There is beyond this earthly tomb
A bright eternity to come!

The Long Man of Bollihope Fell

"Revenge maintains her empire in the breast.
   Though every other feeling freeze to rest;
   And -sooner may the crew-deserted bark,
   When tempests wildly rage and nights are dark,
   Admit a pilot, than may man obtain
   Reason, when toss'd upon the angry main."

— H. Trevanion.

O'er Westerhope, far in the west.
The sun was sinking to his rest
In glorious splendour to behold.
Tinging the clouds with burnished gold,
Which o'er the azure sky above
In wild romantic forms did move.

19

The shrill-toned plover loud did cry,
And becking grouse went whirring by.
Far to the south, o'erspread with trees,
Appeared the distant vale of Tees;
And Shackleborough's rugged height,
In hoary mist, nigh hid from sight;
And, northward, Wear's beauteous dale,
With Bollihope's sweet rural vale;
And, in the background, Rookhope Gill,
With Stanhope Burn and Warden Hill.

Such were the scenes of closing day,
As two men slowly took their way,
Where Bollihope's limpid waters glide.
And climbed the dark-brown mountain side,
Among the moss and waving lirig,
Twixt Polo Pike and Shaftwell Spring.
One was a tail, dark-visaged wight.
Approaching to a giant's height;
His curling locks, of raven hue,
O'erspread his dark and massive brow.
His robust frame, and piercing eyes,
Seem'd fitted for some bold emprise.
The other traveller was but young.
Yet active, vigorous and strong;
His flaxen hair, and ruddy face,
Betoken'd him of Saxon race;
While flashing from his dark-blue eye,
Was purpose bold, and courage high.
As up the mount he did advance,
He often cast a sidelong glance
At his companion, — in the way
As lion fiercely views his prey.

They reached the rugged mountain height,
Where Tees' valley meets the sight;
To rest, they sat down on the bent,
Fatigued by the steep ascent.
Then spoke the dark gigantic man.
And to his comrade thus began: —
"Let us not linger on this height.
Bright Phoebus seeks the shades of night,
The prowling hawk begins to wake,
The timid deer hath sought the brake,

The dusky veil of evening chill
Now spreads around, o'er dale and hill;
Then let us here no longer stay,
But hasten onward on our way."

"Stay!" said the youth, "before we go
I have a secret thou shalt know; —
Before we leave this barren fell,
A tragic story I will tell."
Then, pointing backward, down the vale.
He thus commenced his mournful tale: —

"Down yonder dale, beside that wood,
A humble thatched cottage stood;
There, in that calm sequestered place.
An aged couple passed their days;
Far from all bustle, noise, and strife,
They led a sweet, contented life,
And felt that happy peace of mind
Which higher circles seldom find.
Two children had that honest pair,
A blooming son and daughter fair;
Ellen was their daughter named.
For loveliness and virtue famed.
Her brother Arthur oft would leave
His home and bunt the deer till eve,
For in the chase well was he known.
From Killhope Fell to Stanhope town.

"One night, when fiercely blew the blast,
And rain descended thick and fast,
A stranger to their cottage came;
Hubert, he told them, was his name.
He said he'd travelled far that day,
And on the moor had lost his way.
And strayed o'er deep morasses wide.
Until their cottage he espied.
The old man bade him stay all night.
And journey in the morning light.
And kindly pressed him still to share
With them their homely rustic fare;
Meanwhile, fresh garments they supplied,
And o'er the fire his drench'd clothes dried.
Mirthfully the evening pass'd —

They were delighted with their guest,
And all invited him to stay,
Whene'er again he came that way.
After that, he ne'er forgot
To pay a visit to the cot.

 "Ellen's heart had little rest,
Love's tender flame had touched her breast;
For what had cheered her mind before
Pleased and delighted her no more.
Oft 'neath the elm tree was she known
To sit and meditate alone,
And linger at the twilight hour.
And look for Hubert o'er the moor.
Poor girl! the world she had not prov'd.
She little knew the man she lov'd;
His wickedness to her unknown,
She framed his feelings as her own.
Nor were her parents e'er aware
They entertained a villain there,
Who, like a wolf, rav'nous and bold,
Was scheming how to rob their fold.
Oh! who can paint the dire despair
That did their aged bosoms tear,
When one bright morn they rose from bed
And found their guest and daughter fled;
And though they sought the country round
The fugitives could not be found!
They did not long survive the blow,
Cold death soon eased them of their woe;
And now their earthly toils are past,
Their souls the blessed Virgin rest!

 "Arthur, of home and friends bereft,
His native valley straightway left;
To him it could no pleasure yield, —
He went and sought the battle-field,
In his king and country's cause.
The haughty foreigner to oppose.
Long time he could no tidings hear
Of Hubert and his sister dear;
At length he heard the tidings sad,
His sister Ellen, she was dead!
Had he been able e'er to trace

Her vile seducer, mean and base,
He would have stabb'd him where he stood,-
Wash'd out their woes in his heart's blood!

"Seven long years," he cried, "are past,
The hour I've sought has come at last;
Tm young Arthur, thou must know.
And thou, base villain, art my foe;
Here we meet, in mortal strife, —
Draw thy sword, — defend thy life!"

Then fiercely gleam'd dark Hubert's eye,
As to the youth he did reply, —
"Hast thou come with me on this fell,
Thus an old woman's tale to tell,
And vilely challenge me to fight.
Though I ne'er saw thee till this night?
Thy parents, sister, and their cot,
I tell thee, now, I knew them not!
Then keep thy taunts within thy mouth;
Remember thou art but a youth,
And but for that, I would have soon
With my broad falchion hewn thee down!"

"Base liar! —" said the fair-haired youth;
"Thou stranger to remorse or truth;
Dost thou then think I know thee not,
That thy cursed form could be forgot?
No, wretch! thy face I could have found
Had there been thousands standing round.
Wert thou as tall as yon pine trees
That rustle in the northern breeze.
Yet I would not have been afraid
To combat with thee, blade to blade;
And I will satisfaction have,
Before this mountain-top I leave!"

"Then, by the powers of earth and heaven,
That satisfaction shall be given;
Thou shalt not wait;" thus Hubert spoke,
And at young Arthur dealt a stroke;
But Arthur had the movement spied.
And nimbly dash'd the blade aside;
Then, hand to hand, they both engaged,

And long and fierce the combat raged.
Hubert's wilder passions rose,
And faster still he showered his blows;
And as he on young Arthur pressed.
To end at once the fierce contest,
He in his breast received a wound.
Which struck him, dying, to the ground!

   "Arthur! thou art avenged at last,
I feel life's tide is ebbing fast;
Too long from duty's path I've swerved,
My fate is what I have deserved;
In wickedness my life has past,
And like a wretch I die at last!"

   Upon the turf he dropped his head,
And his immortal spirit fled.

   Early on the ensuing day,
Some travellers chanced to pass that way,
And Hubert's stiffened body found.
And laid it in the mossy ground;
And, now, a grey stone marks the place.
And letters on it you may trace;
And shepherds still the legend tell,
Of the "Long Man of Bollihope Fell!"

Will Toward and the Bailiff

A TRUE STORY

"And as an arrow swiftly flies,
   Shot by an archer strong,
   So did he fly."

— Cowper.

Will Toward was a miner strong;
   No better could be found
To swing a pick, or drive a wedge.
   Or turn a jumper round.

He was, as all his neighbours say,
   A strange, eccentric wight;

Next to good ale, mischief and fun
   Were always his delight

But though he plagu'd his neighbours sore,
   He did not idle stand;
When they had hay to win, or peats.
   He lent a helping hand.

Next door to his a poor man lived,
   With many children small,
And nothing but his daily toil
   For to maintain them all.

And being much involved in debt.
   Which often is the case,
His creditors, quite angry, sent
   A Bailiff to the place.

So to his neighbour. Will, he came,
   A mournful tale he told.
How everything about the house
   Was going to be sold.

"Come, neighbour, cheer up!" said Will,
   "And do not be distrest;
Trust me. I'll very soon find means
   To rid you of your guest."

Then Will began to dress himself
   In a most curious plight,
A blue frock-coat he buttoned up
   Around his body tight.

He had a felt-hat on his head.
   Which was without a crown;
His trousers cut off by the knees,
   His stockings hanging down.

He let his long, dark, matted hair
   Hang down before his eyes;
And with a gully in his belt,
   Complete was his disguise.

And, thus equipped, he straightway to

His neighbour's house did go
Bellowing loudly, as he went in,
   Like a wild buffalo.

The family, as had been plann'd,
   In seeming haste ran out,
While, like a maniac, he began
   To roar and jump about.

He of the Bailiff, who sat still,
   No notice seemed to take.
But howl'd, and bark'd, and yell'd, and did
   A dreadful uproar make.

Sometimes he rolled upon the floor.
   Then hopp'd round like a frog.
Then tore his hat between his teeth.
   Like some ferocious dog.

The Bailiff, of such actions wild
   No good opinion had;
He was convinced, beyond a doubt,
   The man was raving mad!

At length. Will drew his gully forth,
   And fiercely turned about;
The Bailiff bounded from his seat,
   And quickly bolted out.

And down the dale he swiftly ran —
   A frighten'd man was he —
He thought if he overtaken was,
   That he would murder'd be.

And shrieking like an Indian,
   Will swiftly did pursue. —
He had no thought of catching him,
   But keeping him in view!

O'er sikes and brakes away they sped!
   But, pitiful to tell,
Up to the middle in a pool
   The poor Bailiff fell.

But there he did not dally long,
   Out, soon, he had to hop;
Will, with his gully, was nigh hand, —
   There was no time to stop!

Splashing, dashing, on he went.
   As he had done before;
His trousers wet clung to his legs,
   Which did annoy him sore.

Puffing, blowing, like to burst,
   With running nearly spent,
His trembling limbs began to ache.
   Yet onward still he went!

At length he to a farmhouse came,
   And open'd quick the door;
But being tired out and faint,
   He fell down on the floor.

The farmer quickly raised him up,
   And garments fresh supplied,
While his torn, wet, bespattered suit.
   Before the fire he dried.

"Come, tell me, now," the farmer said,
   "Whatever has taken place?
And why you've sprung into my house.
   In such a wretched case?"

"I've just escaped from death," said he;
   "A madman, with his knife.
Has chased me, with the fell intent
   To take away my life!"

The farmer shrewdly guess'd the joke.
   But he was not inclin'd
To tell the man it was a hoax.
   By waggish Will designed.

The Bailiff, next day, took his leave,
   And his course homeward steer'd;
And he in Harwood, from that day,
   Has never more appear'd!

Betty and the Three-Legged Stool

Near Middleton, as old folks tell.
In a thatch'd cot, close to the fell.
Old John and Betty Grey did dwell; —
    As strange a pair
As ever heard a marriage bell,
    Or wedded were.
John, poor man, had as vile a spouse
As ever wore a pair of shoes;
Like Bomba, she held in the house
    Despotic sway;
He, like a poor silly goose,
    Had to obey.

And he a sad time with her spent;
He never could make her content,
Her vile tongue would have vex'd a saint:
    'Twas seldom still;
Click, clack, from mom till night it went.
    Like a corn-mill.

Her husband thus she would provoke.
Or strange tales of her neighbours talk;
And like such idle, stupid folk.
    She could not read,
But she could like a Dutchman smoke
    The nasty weed.

Upon a three-legg'd stool or kit,
Old Betty mostly loved to sit;
The stool had at the top been split,
    For some time past;
Two iron plates were nail'd to it,
    To hold it fast.

But to my tale. One winter's night.
To chat with them came neighbour Wright;
He was a witty humourous wight,
    And loved fun;
The curious tales he could recite
    Pleased every one.

Old Betty had laid down in bed,
Complaining of an aching head;
When Wright went in, to John she said,-
    "Warm me the stool,
And then see that the pig be fed, —
    Be quick, thou fool!"

John did as Betty did desire,
And placed the stool before the fire,
Then went to grunter in the byre.
    Nor durst refuse;
He know whate'er she did require,
    Brook'd no excuse.

But while he on the pig did wait,
Wright placed the stool before the grate.
And held it till each iron plate
    Was nigh red hot.
Then laid it, as John op'd the gate.
    To the old spot.

Poor John came in, — he had no dread
Of the vile trick that Wright had play'd,-
And to his better half he said,
    "The stool is warm;"
Then Betty straightway rose from bed,
    Not dreaming harm.

And down she sat; but up she sprung,
Like as if by a serpent stung;
Like a steam-engine went her tongue;
    John stood dismayed:
She quickly seiz'd the stool, and flung
    It at his head.

With pain -and passion she did roar,
And danc'd and capered on the floor;
She'd ne'er made such a row before, —
    Rais'd was her blood:
Wright and poor John made for the door.
    Fast as they could.

How long her fury did remain,

I never yet could ascertain;
Or how John did the case explain,
        Her wrath to cool: —
I know he ne'er was ask'd again
        To warm a stool.

In fact the stool got out of use;
She would not have it in the house:
Its sight was quite enough to rouse
        Her anger up;
None knew, when once her tongue was loose,
        When it would stop.
I this verse, as a moral, write: —
Women! do not your husbands slight;
Remember Betty on that night,
        How she was smitten:
Bear this in mind, — that those who bite
        Are often bitten!

Gib's Auld Mear

(Local Dialect.)

This was a mare belonging to Gib T_____n, an ore carrier, who had had it upwards of twenty-two years, having brought it up from a foal. , A better nag was never yoked; but being feeble by age and hard work it broke down, while carrying coals to Shamberry mine. The owner loosed it from the cart, and left it lying, and went on his way. Some miners returning from their work, seeing it in such a predicament, raised it from the ground, and conveyed it to Mr. A_____n's. Middle End, who, thinking it was with foal, and that rest and good treatment would soon revive it, begged it of the owner; but his judgment proving to be wrong, he grew tired of keeping an animal which could never be of any use to him, and wanted Gib to pay for its keep, which he refused to do, on the plea that It was a gift. An altercation took place, and a great deal of ill-feeling was displayed on both sides. The poet, therefore, composed this poem, as he was going to work one fine morning.

Upon yan clear September mom,
Az folk were gether'n in tliir com; —
'Twas five o'clock, or varra near,
Az aw unto mie wark did steer;
Mie wallet owre mie shoulder flung.
At a brisk pace aw jogged along;
Aw knew for wark it was quite soon,

Sae 'neath a wall aw sat ma down,
By a plantation et's weel kenn'd,
Near Al_____n's, at Middle End.

While aw was sitting on the ground,
A w heard a strange, unearthly sound;
Aw luk'd around, aw thought it queer,
An' spi'd it was Gib T_____n's auld mear.
Yis, thar it stood — 'twas nae mistak —
An' like a human being spak;
Aw lubb'd mie e'en, for it did seem
It could be naught else but a dream,
But 'twasn't lang before I knew
Et what aw saw and hear'd was true.

"Young man," it said, "you needn't wonder.
For it is real, it is nae blunder;
Don't be surpris'd, or think't a joke,
To hear a poor auld mear talk.
You will hae read what com to pass
When t'prophet Balaam wollop'd t'ass,
How it did open t'jaws sae wide,
An' did its maister straightway chide:
Then cease, young man, to scratch your pate,
While aw to you mie life relate.

"Now two and twenty years hae fled,
Syn aw a little foal was bred,
An' how aw then did sport an' play
Doth seem to me like yisterday.
Oh, how I then did loupe an' trot,
Aw thought mine was a happy lot;
Aw sported free frae care or strife,
An' led an easy plisent life:
Mie plisure ended varra soon.
When aw'd a little aulder grown.

"Aw wasn't lang remaining idle,
Soon to mie head they popp'd a bridle;
Aw gat a t'yaste o' the whup-thong,
Aw had to drag a cart along.
Yis! ivvery day, baith wet an' fine,
Aw had to travel to some mine;
Whinivver they had yur to fill,

31

To tak two bings to Blackton mill; [1]
Frae Calla [2] unto Blackton twice, —
A day like that is nut sae nice.
An' monny a time to Gaundles mill,
An' that's a langer journey still;
Nor com back empty on the road,
For they wi' coal mie cart did load;
But whether carting coals or wood.
Aw always did the best aw could,
An' Gib can prove mie statement well,
If he the truth to you will tell.

"Aw Gib for mie first raaister had,
At first aw thaught he wasn't bad,
But soon aw led a sorry life.
Aw then fond out he'd got a wife;
Then ivvery day aw got weell hather'd.
For Gib, you know, is nobbut [3] natter'd. [4]
Aw was wraught hard az aw could be,
Until at length I strain'd mie knee;
An' now here is a lump sae big,
It's like the blether of a pig.

"The last time aw wi' Gib did go.
Was unto Sharnberry Grove, you know.
To tak some coals, and then to fill
Some yur, to tak to Blackton mill.
Aw fand me strength was failing fast,
Aw thaught grim death had come at last;
Nut a step farther could aw gan,
Which made auld Gib an angry man:
A creeping chillness on me stole,
An' weak and faint aw down did fall,
Then Gibby loos'd me fra the cart,
And then for Shamberry he did start,
And left me on the ground to lie.
At length some grovers did come by,
Then from the ground they did ma raise,
Wi' monny a gry'an an' monny a paza

"Aw then to Al____n was given,
Aw hae wi' him syn then been living;
But he would not had me at all.
But that he thaught aw was wi' foal.

What they intend to do wi' me,
Is mair than aw can tell to thee;
But still az thinking, varra soon.
For t'squire's dogs they'll tak ma down;
Nae matter what they do wi' me
Aw nobbut hae but yance to dee.

"Aw forgive auld Gib wi' all mie heart,
Aw oft see him gan by wi' t'cart;
Aw think he hae's sair croppen in,
Aw 'magine he lukes varra thin.
He'll be like t'rest o' t'human race
When they hae nigh spun out thir days^
Who hae stern poverty to 'bide,
Who, like auld clouts, are thrown aside."
Aw thaught aw wad say a word or twee;
A.W says, — "Auld mear, we don't agree:
Aw really think it cannot be
    What ye've last tauld,
That men hae naught but poverty
    When they git auld;
For there are clubs et de provide
For men, when they're wi' sickness tried;
Therefore, don't think they're thrawn aside,
    To fend or f'yal,
For they can tell the world wide
    A different t'yal."

Up again, then, spak t'auld mear;
It said, — "Aw's varra glad to hear
Et thar's something to keep a man,
When labour he nae langer can,
Et he may nivver feel distress,
Therefore, I wish the club success!
But az for me, syn wark is pass'd,
Aw've had to suffer the keen blast
O' monny a cauld an' stormy day
Without a bite o' corn or hay;
An Al____n does begrudge mie meat,
Although it's little et aw eat.
For it he's wanted Gib to pay,
Though aw to him was gi'en away.
He needn't be sae discontent,
For aw get nought frae him but bent;

Aw sometimes think it may be that
Et maks Gib ne'er come whar aws at;
Sec things as that sud nivver vex him,
But whiles, aw think, ez conscience pricks em.
But while that aw has life an' bluid,
Aw'll think o' Jack [5] wi' gratitude.
Last winter, monny a stormy day,
He braught to me baith com an' hay;
Aw wish em luck while he does live,
An' all my foes aw do forgive;
An' in whativver shape comes death,
Aw's riddy to resign mie breath;
Aw lang wi' death mie limbs to rest,
To me 'tis nae unwelcome guest."

This was the t'yal el t'mear telt me.
An' it's az true az it can be;
Aw left it thar the bent to swallow,
While aw mov'd on mie way to Calla;
But when aw e'er by t'plantation steer.
Aw still remember "Gib's auld Mear."

[1] Smelt mill.   [2] California or Little Egglestrope Mine.
        [3] Only.   [4] Ill-natured.   [5] Gib's Brother.

The Fells

I dearly love the mountain, for 'tis there
Dame Nature in her wildest form appears;
The purple waving heath, the brooklet's sheen,
The mossy swamps, and hoary cliffs adorned
With bilberry shrubs and graceful ferns, —
All have their pleasing charms for me. Oft have I
At the mine shop door, at early morn,
Stood, as the rising orb of day-
Was peering o'er the eastern horizon,
Tinging with gold the mountain tops.
Watching the becking grouse, as they each other chas'd
In sportive play; and merry, soaring lark,
As from its dewy bed it mounted high.
Carolling sweetly as it rose, till like
A speck it seem'd amid the downy clouds,
Blending its lively song with the shrill notes
Of plover and curlew, and the hoarse croak

Of the dark raven sailing in the air,
And scanning with anxious eyes the ground
For the dead carcase of some sheep, to ease
The pressing cravings of a hungry crop.
Thus have I spell-bound stood, until my mind
To darker bygone days has wandered back,
When stranger scenes appeared to the eye,
And stranger sounds rose on the mountain breeze, —
Sounds of fierce men in deadly combat met,
Like tigers thirsting for each other's blood; —
When Douglas and Randolph the border cross'd
With brave and hardy followers mounted well
On nimble steeds, well train'd to pace the moss,
And burning to avenge the many wrongs
Their country suffered from our hands, over
The peaty swamps they rode and like a flood
They swept the vales below, and left behind
A blackened scene of woe to mark their track.
How thankful should we be that such fierce broils
No more disgrace our isle, and that in peace
Both nations were united in a bond
Of brotherhood, and bound together with
A Gordian knot, — a happy junction,
Which by the sword could never have been wrought.
Since then, how swiftly has our isle progressed
In knowledge, power, and in enterprise!
How has the aspect of the landscape chang'd!
I still can trace the ancient path, with bent
And stunted ling o'ergrown, which formerly
Was the chief way across the mountains bleak
From Teesdale high unto the river Wear,
Where from Newcastle merchandise was brought,
Pack'd up in sacks, strapped on to ponies' backs;
The drivers drest in thick, warm, home-spun coats,
Arm'd always to the teeth; for well they knew
That danger in their path did often lurk.
Fierce banditti did the mountains sore infest,
And from their hiding places they rush'd forth,
And stopp'd the travellers journeying past;
Vilely stripped them, and left them almost nak'd
Their journey to pursua But times have chang'd; —
No more those bloody villains pace the moss;
Justice, once tardy in her steps, moves now
With stride more rapid in the path of crime.

Pack horses now no longer bring our goods, —
They now are swiftly whirl'd on iron rails
From place to place, by steam's strong agency;
And news from distant parts is borne on wires,
Swift as the lightning passes through the sky,
So that we now can conversation hold
With all the nations round about. Could I
Look forward but two hundred years, what strange
Things should I see! Perhaps as great a change
Will have been wrought as has been since this moor
Was one vast forest, where stately oak trees
Flourished and spread wide their giant limbs,
Whose trunks now lie embedded in the moss.
Perhaps tall trees again may rear their heads,
And fields of yellow grain wave in the breeze,
Instead of rushes, bent, and ling. Though wild
The scenery be, — and wilder still when
Winter resumes his regal sway, and keenly
The bitter, frosty wind doth pierce the frame.
And thick and fast descends the fleecy snow,
No flower or blade of grass to meet the eye, —
Yet to a Briton's heart 'tis dearer far
Than all the spicy, fragrant orange groves,
Where beauteous flowers perfume the air,
Which Spain and sunny Italy can boast.
Though bleak our native hills, yet they are free!
For Britain is by Britons only ruled;
And may it still continue so! May the
Supreme, who holds the nations in His hand.
Still watch o'er and protect our native isle.
May noble, virtuous hearts be rear'd still.
To guard our shores 'gainst the invading foe, —
Men who revere their country and their God.

To "Onlooker."

"But what has become of Richard Watson— Is his lyre broken?"
                              "Onlooker." — Teesdale Meboubt.

   "The fire in the bosom of Etna concealed,
    Still mantles unseen In its secret recess."

                         — BYRON.

Rous'd by "Onlooker's" kind remarks,
   I cannot well refrain

From bringing to the light my muse,
   And courting her again.
Let fellow dalesmen not suppose
My rhyming days are at a close,
   Or weak has turned my muse:
Nor bent nor broken is my lyre;
As bright and tuneful is each wire
   As when 'twas first in use.
My mind still, inclined still
   To sing some cheerful lay;
It lightens and brightens
   Life's rugged dreary way.

Though the sweet valley of the Tees
   I've had to leave behind,
Yet are the scenes I loved so well
   Engraven on my mind.
Each flowery dell, each hazel wood,
Each waterfall, each rushing flood.
   And limpid mountain rill,
Still, still to my mind's eye appear
Their outlines as distinct and clear
   As if I viewed them still,
Those views still, infuse still
   Warm thoughts, and pleasure give,
Intruding, deluding —
   By them I cannot live.

Toss'd up and down as I have been,
   On life's rough stormy main;
Crushed with a load of care, and bound
   By poverty's strong chain.
Exposed to many a hard rebuff,
Ills which I fear are quite enough
   To sour the mind sometimes.
And cause me to lay down the pen,
And leave to more untrammelled men
   Our local songs and rhymes.
Who chooses the muses.
   If poor, lacks not woe;
Subjected, neglected,
   Till death has brought him low.

I'm told I've many friends who love

My rhymes and songs to read,
I know I've friends, and staunch ones too.
    Yet they are few indeed.
And thankful am I for that few.
They fall like kind, refreshing dew,
    On ground parched hard and dry;
They fan the sparks of latent fire,
And lead my spirit to aspire
    To things more strong and high.
Completely, and sweetly,
    The powers of friendship move.
Combining, entwining,
    Our hearts by cords of love.

In Baldwin, pleased am I to see
    Another of the trade,
I know well he has all the parts
    Of which a bard is made.
Long may he strike his native lyre
With stirring, true poetic fire,
    And keep on climbing still,
With modest grace and steady aim,
The upward path that leads to fame,
While I descend life's hill.
May pleasure, in measure
    Not scanty, on him flow,
Each blessing possessing
    A rural bard can know.

The Two Ill-Favoured Ones

Returning yam frae wark yan neet,
Plodding alang wi' weary feet,
While the full mune's pale borrowed leet
    M'yad objects near,
As if t'been day, luke ti my seet
    Distinct and clear.
Aw at the village had ti wait,
Which put ma on my journey late;
It's nae Strang drink was i' my pate
    To lead ma wrang,
Though tir'd eneugh, at nae slaw rate
    Aw jogged alang.

By the roadside aw chanced to see
Two tramps, ensconc'd beneath a tree,
Ill-luiking as they weel could be, —
    This was my thought,
They mean nae good, their luik shows me
    They'll stick at nought.

Yan was a chap, loose, lang, and lean,
Wi' shriveird face, and hollow een,
Yan hungrier luiking aw'd ne'er seen,
    Or mair distressed,
Clad in thin rags, not ower clean,
    Sae was he dressed.

The other was amaist as bad,
An' luik'd as if he'd been half-mad;
His countenance was grim an' sad,
    An' quite care-worn.
As if he nivver had been glad
    Sen he was born.

To them wi' little fear aw went,
Thought aw, if they're on robbing bent,
Their time wie me'll be ill-spent,
    A useless job,
Because on me aw'd not a cent
    For them to rob.

Said they, "We hae but little care
Whar we may lodge, or how we fare,
In fact we're dreaded ivverywhere,
    By heigh an' low;
Depend on't we're nae welcome pair,
    Reet weel we know.

"That we're ill company we grant,
Whar vice abounds we maistly haunt,
And whar we gan we misery plant,
    An' bring men low;
You've heard of us — my name is Want,
    And this is Woe!

"Dunna be in a stew," said they,

"But seldom we a visit pay
To sober working men, though they
　　Be not weel set.
Who hae to toil hard ivvery day
　　Their bread to get.

"It tries a poor man's utmost skill
To find grist for the household mill.
When he's got mony mouths to fill.
　　And claes find, too;
But, if he careful be, he will
　　Get foughten through.

"Wi' them et frae their duty shrink,
And of the future nivver think,
But waste their means on madd'ning drink.
　　We often dwell,
An' push them onward to the brink
　　O' death an' hell.
"An' sec as them et wander wide
Frae Christian truth, without a guide,
An' set religion quite aside.
　　An' live in sin,
To these we soon become allied.
　　An' enter in.

"If mortals will plain truth oppose,
An' their ears to good counsel close,
And wilfully break Nature's laws,
　　An' yam neglect,
Of their own ills they are the cause,
　　We the effect.

"Dunnot think the rich are free, although
Of me they do but little know,
Whar evil is, my brother Woe
　　Is on the track:
Not all the money they can show
　　Can keep him back.

"If mankind would act as they should.
And work for yan another's good.
United in a brotherhood,
　　This fact is clear,

From their domestic hearths we would
   Soon disappear.

"But we'll be moving, time rolls by,
Our avocations we mun ply;
Our presence will cause mony a sigh
   Ere morning leet."
"An' aw'll be gannen, too," said I,
    "Good neet, good neet."

The Weasel and the Mouse

Returning homeward from the town,
One sultry July afternoon,
I, in a shady place, sat down,
   Near Park End Wood,
Where once a hamlet of renown
   Named Unthank stood.
Here massive crags lie by the way,
Coated with moss and lichens grey;
Where graceful ferns and foxgloves gay,
   Profusely grow:
Nature does here in bright array
   Her beauties show.

Another scene soon caught my eye,
A little mouse ran scampering by,
Though scarcely knowing where to fly,
   Oft glancing back;
As if some dreadful foe was nigh.
   And on its track.

I puzzled was awhile, to know
What made the beast run too and fro, —
Although its actions wild did show
   It was in dread;
Till, near me, I a weasel saw
   Uprear its head.

The vicious vermin looked around,
It saw the mouse, and, with a bound,
Skipped o'er the hard uneven ground
   With rapid stride:

The mouse received a fatal wound,
   And squeaking died!

I rose the savage brute to slay.
But was to late, it quit its prey,
And darted 'mong the rocks away.
   To save its skin;
I might as well 'mong stacks of hay
   Have sought a pin.

I sat down, and to think began. .
How strange, thought I, is Nature's plan!
How numerous are the powers which can
   Nip out life's breath;
The bestial tribes and even man
   Must live by death.

I need not wander far to find
Men just as viciously inclined
As any of the weasel kind, —
   Plain truth to speak;
Who, to all but self interest blind,
   Would crush the weak.

Some to the mouse are near allied,
When they're with sore affliction tried
Become confused — nor can decide
   Which way to steer,
They sink exhausted in the tide
   Of grief and fear!

Others there are, and not a few,
Who nothing definite pursue;
And, with no end or aim in view,
   Move too and fro
Till poverty becomes their due,
   And brings them low.

While many spend life's fleeting hour
In pleasure's fascinating power,
And the best traits of manhood lower,
   Nor think to slack —
While, like the weasel, ruin sure
   Is on their track.

Grim death relentless tracks our way,
To it we'll all become a prey;
Let us prepare so that we may.
    When it draws near.
Quit this frail tenement of clay
    Without a fear.

The Biters Bitten

A TRUE STORY.

Gib Tom and Robin Allinson,
    In Teesdale were known well;
They carriers were, and neighbours too,
    And did at Skears dwell.
And each a stud of ponies kept,
    Brought from the Highland hills,
To take the lead ore from the mines,
    Unto the smelting mills.
Stout, hardy, well-built men were they,
    Fit to stand any weather;
And as their business was the same,
    They often went together.
But they were vain and quarrelsome,
    And very ill-tongued too;
At fairs and at elections were
    The cause of many a row.

And often they were heard to say.
    No two men of the place,
In an encounter with the fist,
    They were afraid to face.
But 'tis a saying true that those
    Who love to fight and fratch.
Have never far to go before
    They fall in with their match.

As they passed Stotley Carse one day,
    A tinker they espied,
Stretch'd fast asleep upon the grass
    That grew by the roadside
Said Tom to Rob, "We'll have some fun,

43

We have no fear of blows;
We'll steal up to him while he sleeps.
    And we will pull his nose."

The plan pleased Robin, who would not
    At silly actions stick;
"We'll prove the tinker's pluck," said he,
    "'Twill be a clever trick."
For certainly so large a nose
    They'd never seen before;
And, like a trumpet's martial blast.
    Loud did the tinker snore.

They softly went up to the man,
    Unwitting of his foes;
Tom laid his hand upon his face,
    And seized him by the nose.
When the rude grasp the tinker felt.
    He sprang up with a bound;
And by a well directed blow,
    Fell'd Gib Tom to the ground.

And, quick as lightning, turning round.
    He did Gib's partner meet;
And Rob, with all his boasting, soon
    Lay breathless at his feet
Tom soon recovered, and arose
    The conflict to maintain;
'Twas to receive another blow
    Which sent him down again.

And, also, Robin in his turn
    Had the same fate to share;
That they had caught a Tartar fierce
    Too late they were aware.
The tinker o'er his fallen foes,
    Stood calm with watchful eyes;
To strike them to the ground whene'er
    They did attempt to rise.

Batter'd and bruis'd and vanquished by
    His crushing heavy fist;
With shame they had to own their fault,
    And beg him to desist

"You¹ve had enough," said he, "and learned
  With tinkers not to fight;
You played a foolish joke on me,
  And I have served you right.

"Go on your way, and be more wise.
  And this advice give I;
Whene'er you see a sleeping dog,
  Pass on and let it lie."

Evening Meditations

**While sitting near the old church of St. Mart, Middleton-in-Teesdale, short-
ly before it was pulled down, to make room for one of larger dimensions, to
meet the requirements of the greatly increased population of the district.**

Our ancient church, which could withstand,
Years yet to come, Time's crumbling hand;
The noblest relic of our town
Will soon we hear be levell'd down.
And, in its stead, a new one rais'd
More suited to the modern taste.
'Tis right enough our fancies should
Succumb, when for the public good
Old things must pass away, but yet
We'll view its downfall with regret;
Thoughts of the past unbidden rise.
Which bind our hearts, by various ties,
To those familiar stone walls grey.
Ne'er to be loosed till life gives way.
Here our forefathers worshipped God,
One only path they knew or trod;
No party feelings did them move —
Too often felt opposed to love
By narrow minds, when it is known
Opinions differ from their own.
No silly pride in dress they had.
They were in thick warm garments clad,
Which from their fleecy flocks they won.
And in long winter ev'nings spun.
Unlike some, now-a-days, attired
In gaudy clothes to be admir'd;
Though somewhat rude and unrefined,
Yet were hospitable and kind,
45

Aiding each other when in need,
With hearts unswayed by selfish greed;
Nor thought to claim remuneration
For every little obligation.
For others' sorrows they could feel,
Nor ever grudged to give a meal
To the wayfaring stranger poor.
Who weary wandered to their door.
. Such were our ancestors, we're told,
Who sat in this quaint building old;
Can we, their offspring, truly say
We are much better men than they?
In this same church my parents good.
Blithely before the altar stood —
Both in the bloom and prime of life.
To be united man and wife.
They with hearts hopeful, free, and light,
Would deem this world an Eden bright;
For youthful joys and pleasure hide
The aspect of it's darker side.
A faithful, upright pair they proved.
And warmly they each other lov'd;
Working with prudence and forethought-
Life's battle hard they bravely fought
I've heard how gay they were that mom
I, their strange rhyming son was born;
Indulging in displays of fun
Because I was their first-born son.
Within this ancient structure, soon,
They took me to John Henry Brown,
Our Rector good, for learning famed,
By whom I was baptized and named.
But not for classic lore alone
Was this respected pastor known;
A generous heart beat in his breast,
He sought the needy and distress'd;
Relieving them whene'er he could
With cash and clothes, medicine and food;
And did true merit patronise.
Aiding the talented to rise —
Bringing their latent powers forth;
In fact, men knew not half his worth.
Because he wish'd no trumpet blown
To let his generous deeds be known.

When Nature's beauties struck my mind,
And for the muse I felt inclin'd,
He got me books — with useful rules
For poetiy, taught in high schools;
Anxious this knowledge to impart,
He gave me tasks to learn by heart;
A critic true — he was not slow
In pointing out the slightest flaw;
Though at such times he would appear
Somewhat too rigorous and severe,
Yet still, I fancied all the while,
I could discern a lurking smile,
But his kind acts came to an end —
He's gone, and I have lost a friend;
Gone too are my kind parents dear,
I see their resting place from here;
To me a hallow'd sacred spot,
One which can never be forgot!
When on earth's scenes I close my eye,
Here I would wish my bones to lie!
Vain thought perhaps, — God only knows
Where this old fabric shall repose!
No matter where the framework lies —
It changes not what never dies.
The sun has gone down in the west;
The noisy rooks in quiet rest;
From the day's slumber bats awake.
And homeward I my way must take, —
For eight the hammer strikes the bell:
House of my ancestors! Farewell!

The Approach of Winter

The yellow leaves fall from the trees,
Strewn on the ground by every breeze
    That now more chilly blows;
No longer songs of birds we hear,
Their warbling, till another year.
    Did with the summer close;
Fast fading are the lovely flowers.
    Those gems that please the eye.
The face of Nature plainly shows
    Stern winter drawing nigh;
    When rudely and loudly.

47

The bitter north winds blow;
  Lifting and drifting.
In heaps, the powdery snow.
Dire season! Numerous toilers poor,
Ill set thy tempests to endure,
  With fear thy coming view;
While trade is slack throughout the land,
Labour's supply exceeds demand,
  And want and woe ensue;
Parents their half-starv'd offspring see
  Ill clad in garments old,
Too scanty, and too thin by far.
  To keep them from the cold;
  Dejected, affected
With ills they cannot mend;
  Like rushes, or bushes.
They to the storms must bend.

O hope! that sweetens sorrow's cup,
And, on life's rough sea, bears us up
  From sinking 'neath the tide;
Still cheer us with thy heavenly light,
Be not o'ercast, or take thy flight,
  But in our hearts abide:
Direct our minds from earth's dull scenes
  To bright unclouded skies,
Where peace has everlasting sway.
  And tempests never rise;
  No tears there, no fears there,
'Tis the home of the blest.
  No sadness, all gladness,
Tis there the weary rest.

To Delta

**In answer to a paragraph which appeared in the Teesdale Mercury, where
he eulogized the writings of "T'Licen'd Hawker" and "The Poet," and en-
quired why the latter delayed in bringing out a book of his works before
the public.**

Mr. Editor.

Dear Sir, I'll be obliged to you
If you will kindly space allow
Me, in your columns, to reply

Unto a paragraph, which I
Saw in your issue of last week.
Where Delta does so warmly speak
In praise of "T'Licen'd Hawker's" notes,
And of my sentiments and thoughts.
I, therefore, have this letter penn'd,
To thank our generous-hearted friend;
We feel encouraged, and at ease.
When we're inform'd our writings please;
"T'Licen'd Hawker" all declare.
Of genius has an ample share;
Our dalesmen do not hesitate
To say his writings are first-rate:
Writ, in the lingo of the dale.
To please your readers cannot fail.
Those who skip o'er and do not heed them.
But then perhaps they cannot read them:
Go on, brave "Hawker" I will say,
In your own curious pleasant way,
And the same satisfaction give,
And long and happy may you live!
As for myself, this I can say,
I'm kept hard going every day —
Still filling up my leisure time
In writing prose and strings of rhyme:
And, if God spares me, I've no doubt
I'll manage soon to bring them out.
A man who toils hard for his bread
Can not so quickly go ahead.
A locomotive moves but slow,
Hard laden, when the steam is low;
Have patience, friend, awhile, and I
Will get the steam up by and by.
By Tweed, Clyde, Ayr, and Doon, I've been,
And lovely places I have seen;
But no place could my fancy please,
Like the sweet valley of the Tees!
Yet Teesdale's harp remains unstrung,
No bard has of its beauties sung, —
Then let the task be yours and mine,
To make it, like the others, shine!
Two years ago, my hope seem'd vain
Of seeing Teesdale's hills again,
When in the hospital I lay

In pain, and restless night and day.
No sympathising friend was there!
Strangers my fellow sufferers were.
Soldiers and weavers of the town,
And sailors bent and broken down.
Who had stood many a stormy blast.
But had come there to breathe their last.
Four months in that place I remained
Till I my wonted strength regain'd;
Being informed, by doctors there,
That I required a change of air,
I threw all drugs and lotions by,
Southward I turn'd, and here am I!
In a straightforward path I'll tread,
Not by contending parties led,
Nor by an enemy cast down;
Nor court a smile, nor fear a frown.
And to this plan I'll ever stick,
Yours, very truly, Poet Dick.

The Solitary Mountain Ash

Tree of the wilds, with spreading boughs.
Blooming alone on this bleak ground,
By the burnside, where heather grows!
A contrast deep thy verdure shows
To the dark, barren aspect round.

Vigorous and fresh, and fair to see,
As are the trees down in the vale.
In the rich soil of a green lea,
Fix'd snugly — not exposed like thee
To every stormy mountain gale.

Many a bitter, wintry blast,
    Rushing with fury in its course
Across the frozen snow-clad waste.
Has tried thy strength; yet still thou hast
    For years withstood their blighting force

When Spring's warm genial days appear,
    And thou in thy green robe art drest,
The cuckoo's notes I often hear

Proceed from thee, distinct and clear,
  Awaking joy within the breast.

Sometimes the raven's croaking cry
  Is heard from out thy foliage gay;
And other birds, that to thee fly,
Often their vocal powers try
  From morning to the close of day.

From thy appearance in this place,
  Thus isolated from thy kind,
I think we may a moral trace
Applicable unto our race,
  A lesson we should bear in mind.

Many a man is placed, we know.
  Where kindred spirits are not found;
Yet blooms, and does his true worth show
'Mong barren minds, 'mid natures low,
  Like thee upon this desert ground.

The man that nobly perseveres
  In duty's path, though it be hard.
With conscience clear, cares not, nor fears
Weak lesser mortals' envious jeers.
  At last will gain his due reward.

And, when life's pilgrimage is o'er,
  He'll leave behind all grief and pain;
Transplanted to a brighter shore,
To bloom in joy for evermore,
  Where pleasures everlasting reign.

On Seeing a Blackbird Lying Frozen and Dead on the Snow

Poor sable-feathered warbler sweet!
No more thy songs shalt thou repeat,
Within the budding grove to greet
  The welcome Spring;
Thou liest, stricken, at my feet —
  A lifeless thing!

How light thy body is, and lean!
Hunger and cold, ills stern and keen
Have thy relentless slayers been,
   I plainly see;
More of thy tribe, this storm, I we'en.
   Will fall like thee.

Some thoughtless men, to reasoning deaf,
Will say thou wast a garden thief.
Though 'tis the naturalist's belief
   Thou wast a friend:
I think so too, and view with grief
   Thy mournful end.

Often, with hungry crop, thou hast
A cheerless night of sorrow past,
As, through the woods, the fleecy blast
   Howl'd, sigh'd, and moan'd:
Not knowing where to break thy fast
   When daylight dawn'd.

Though I'm hard pressed, and very poor,
Yet, hadst thou come unto my door,
I would have from my scanty store
   A few crumbs spared
For thee, till wintry stonns were o'er
   And fields were bared.

But thou with all thy race art shy;
Ye view mankind with jealous eye:
With reason too, I'll not deny.
   This truth I hold,
More birds the gun has caused to die
   Than has the cold.

In these times painful things take place,
Thine is no solitary case —
Some thousands of the human race
   Like woes bewail;
The languid frame and shrunken face
   Tell misery's tale.

Old England, country of my birth.
The greatest nation on the earth —

What heroes have from thee sprung forth,
   Of sword and pen!
Yet, what is all thy glory worth
   To starving men?

May blessings rest on those who plan
Aid for the poor wreck'd working man,
Who nobly do the best they can
   His woes to heal!
We leave alone the selfish clan
   With hearts of steel

Poor bird, adieu! I'll not repine,
Although, perhaps thy fate is mine;
The great all seeing power divine,
   Shall be my stay;
He yet may cause the sun to shine
   On my dark way!

The Wasps' Nest

'Twas on a pleasant summer's day,
When the sweet smell of new-made hay
Was borne upon the Western breeze,
That gently wav'd the forest trees,
When Bob and John, two miners stout,
A-rambling up the dale set out;
Knowing their weekly occupation
Required fresh air and recreation,
They wandered 'mong the rocks and bowers,
Where grow the rarest ferns and flowers;
Above the hamlet of Bowlees,
Where picturesque Winch Bridge spans the Tees.
Here lovers of the muse will find
Something to interest the mind;
Geologists and florists too,
Their favorite studies may pursue.
But our adventurers were not there,
The feelings of such men to share;
They knew of such things, so to speak,
As much as donkeys know of Greek.
Bob sat down, his short pipe to smoke,
While his companion took a walk
Among the shady trees, to find

53

A walking stick to suit his mind.
Bob was not suffered to proceed
In the enjoyment of his weed,
'Ere John's loud voice smote on his ear,
Exclaiming, "Bob! Come here, come here."
He soon was at his comrade's side —
"What's up," said he; when John replied,
"Look up the trunk of this fir tree
And you a swarm of bees will see.
They are, as sure as I'm alive,
A casting from some neighbouring hive
And will delicious honey make,
They are a prize, and no mistake."
"Well, well," said Bob, "you may be right.
Though what I know of bees is slight.
And such as these I never saw;
They may be wild, for ought we know."
"Pooh, pooh," said John, "wild bees indeed!
Say rather, of an improved breed;
They're ours, and therefore we'll contrive
To get them safely in a hive.
Howgill is near, and I'm sure
We there can what we want procure,
And if you here awhile will stay,
I'll go, and not be long away."
So saying, on his errand bent,
Like a roused hare, away he went.
Nor did Bob long alone remain,
John, sweating, soon came back again
With a new straw hive snug and nice,
And rum and sugar, to entice
The insect tribe to quit the tree,
So that they well secured might be.
To make things sure, he also brought
One Hutch, a beekeeper of note,
Who saw how matters stood at once,
When up the tree he took a glance.
As he wished not to spoil the joke.
He, smiling, to the greenhorns spoke —
"You are right lucky men indeed!
This swarm is of a noted breed.
But newly introduced, and rare.
And therefore must be treat with care.
They're named "Hornetta Rega Lascar,"

Brought from the Isle of Madagascar.
Stand back! I think t'would be as well
Let them the rum and sugar smell,
Which, when they taste, they'll be so glad
They'll rush into the hive like mad."
With these remarks he took his leave.
And went off, laughing in his sleeve.
Long did the silly men remain
Watching beside the tree in vain.
Until the evening's dusky veil
Began to spread o'er hill and dale.
Perplexed, and in no pleasant mood.
They cursed the stupid insect brood,
Which showed no sign or inclination
To enter their new habitation.
As deeper grew the shades of night,
Patience became exhausted quite.
On a new plan they did agree,
Which was to knock down from the tree
The paper bag, which held the swarm,
With a long stick. Not dreading harm.
Their folly soon they had to rue.
When out the angry insects flew,
Stinging severely left and right.
Which quickly put the two to flight.
Some shelter from their wrath to gain.
Roaring, as well they might, with pain.
With swollen faces, almost blind,
Leaving their new bought hive behind,
They took their way home past Bowlees,
Well cured of their desire for bees.
Who can their shame and chagrin show
When in due time they came to know
That all their care and toil not small
Was for a wasp's nest after all?
From this adventure we may find,
A moral we should bear in mind;
Ne'er to be too quick to take in hand
Things we do not well understand.
Nor by appearances be led.
Look to the character instead.
Beauty is pleasing when we find
 'Tis with good qualities combined;
But where it is the only charm

Be careful! it may lead to harm.
A pretty face and figure can
Too oft, beguile a thoughtless man;
What suits his eye, contents his mind,
To numerous faults completely blind.
Thus led, he is not satisfied
Till to his fancy he's allied.
He marries; and he lives to see
He's got a wasp and not a bee!

On Catching a Rat in a Trap

Ha, Mr. Rat, I've got thee fast,
Securely in my trap at last!
Many a weary night thou hast
    Disturbed my rest
Now all thy peevish pranks are past
    Thou wicked pest.

Mercy thou shalt not find in me.
Nothing to merit it I see.
I'll take thy life, and thus be free
    From thy aquaintance.
I know, in such a wretch as thee,
    There's no repentance.

Of all the vicious vermin breed.
Noted for thievery and greed,
I think ye rats have quite the lead
    Throughout the nation.
Above all ye are held, indeed.
    In detestation.

For dirty habits ye're renowned,
In filthy sewers ye abound;
From you, our mines beneath the ground
    Are seldom free.
Even in vessels ye are found,
    Out on the sea.

The farmer's crops ye often mar;
With you, he holds continual war.
His riddled corn stacks show you are
    A plague complete.

And what is worse, ye waste, by far.
    More than ye eat.

And ye are cannibals, I'm told.
Strong ones devour the weak and old.
When numerous, ye wax fierce and bold.
    And will defy
Even man, when run into a hold.
    And at him fiy.

Your scratching noise, oft in the night.
Makes many a superstitious wight
Shiver and shake in bed with fright.
    His silly fears
Lead him to think some ghost or sprite
    Is what he hears.

Though to vile habits ye've inclined,
Yet, in the walks of life, we find
Rats plenty, of a two legged kind.
    As bad as you.
To all chief christian virtues blind,
    To friends untrue.

Our Eats political are those
Who discontent and misery cause.
And speak hard things of state and laws,
    Quite out of season,
And lead the ignorant to suppose
    Abuse is reason.

Lit'rary Bats vain light things write,
And fact, for sake of fiction slight.
They get up stories to excite
    The giddy throng.
And oft place characters in a light
    They know is wrong.

The Critic Rats are those who tear
Another's works, and lay them bare.
Even what's good they will not spare.
    And feel no shame.
This seems to be their only care —
    Acquiring fame.

We've also Rats who pray and preach,
And the way unto Heaven teach;
Yet will deceive and overreach
    For worldly gain.
To Mammon they stick like a leech,
    And own his reign.

Poets and rhymers are rats when,
Through motives mean, they verses pen
In praise of undeserving men.
    Of little worth;
Whose minds are weak, yet proud and vain
    Of wealth and birth.

Lawyers are rats when they through greed,
Will against truth and justice plead.
Mean-hearted men of every creed,
    Who manhood lack,
With snobs and swells, are rats indeed;
    And every quack.

And traps there are to catch mankind.
With many tempting baits designed
To fascinate the carnal mind.
    By Satan set.
Who turn aside to taste them, find
    They're in a net.

To Heaven may each hard tempted one
Look up, for aid those snares to shun.
With these remarks my speech is done,
    I must not wait:
So, Mr. Rat, thy race is run,
    Now take thy fate.

Wemmergill

How pleasantly the hall of Wemmergill
Stands, 'mid tall trees, screened by a sloping hill —
The noblest mansion in Lune's pleasant dale,
Where beauty reigns, and rustic joys prevail.
Westward, from springs high up the mountain fed,

A limpid brook flows o'er a limestone bed;
By verdant banks and trees, oft hidden quite —
Anon, appearing in the broad sunlight.
Whose lucid beams make it like silver gleam.
Till, mingling in Lune's larger moss-tinged stream.
How changed is Wemmergill, since last I saw
Its pleasant grounds, nigh fourteen years ago;
I thought they then combined a lovely scene.
But ten times more so do they now, I ween.
Here, graceful ferns their rarest beauties show.
And flowers from every clime profusely grow;
And pleasant gravel walks, 'mong shrubberies green.
Where, in full play, a crystal fount is seen.
Delighted, we admire the taste and mind
Of him, by whom those beauties were designed;
Struck with this Eden, most, because it stands.
In such deep contrast to surrounding lands:
Like some sweet oasis, remote and bright,
'Mid a wild desert, dreary to the sight,
From Mickle Fell's high towering, rocky crest.
Dark, barren mountains stretch along the west —
And southward lie allotments, bleak and poor.
Reclaimed from Kelton's wild, unsheltered moor.
Eastward, Lune, winding, rolls by meads and trees,
Down a romantic valley to the Tees.
And to the north, the Standard mountain lies.
Where Harrigill and Arngill take their rise;
And rude, unhewn, grey, time-worn pillars stand,
Like giant sentinels, to guard the land:
Where beacon fires once blazed, seen from afar,
Which roused the dalesmen for the shock of war —
'Gainst wicked, plundering raiders from the north,
Who o'er the hills to seize the flocks came forth.
But those dire times of border strife are fled.
Even chivalry, they tell us, now is dead.
They say that gentlemen of modern days.
Are a vain, sordid, mercenary race;
Wanting the courage and the martial fire.
Which did their ancestors of yore inspire.
Mistaken words! Let men say what they will,
We have the spirit of true Britons still!
And here, in this sequestered dale we find
One of those gentlemen of "noble" kind;
Of liberal principles, as firm as rock.

One of the noted good old English stock —
No grovelling churl but a stout man of worth.
An honour to the land which gave him birth;
Not, monklike, living in dull sluggish ease.
Our active field sports best his fancy please.
With dog and gun disporting many an hour.
No better marksman ever paced a moor.
Not for self solely living, as some do —
He seeks to make those round him happy too,
To all our dalesmen, loyal and sincere,
Long will the name of Mil bank be held dear.
See! gathering round on this gay festal eve,
A token of his kindness to receive,
A swelling multitude; in which we trace
Pleasure and joy depicted in each face.
Here, hoary dalesmen leaning on their sticks,
With happy schoolboys full of vigour, mix;
And laughing maidens, rear'd where bleak winds blow.
Whose rosy cheeks with health and beauty glow.
Unto a spacious tent, they soon draw near
And seat themselves; enjoy the goodly cheer.
In this gay throng, by all admired the most,
Are the fair, sprightly daughters of the host;
With easy grace, from place to place they glide.
Free from all foolish pageantry and pride.
With the same grace they'll mount a fiery steed.
And dash o'er the rough moor at racing speed.
But nobler qualities than these they show —
Oft to the houses of the poor they'll go;
Soothing the sick, relieving the distress'd.
Infusing joy into the joyless breast
By such acts in their parent's steps they move.
Winning the country's high esteem and love.
Thus, mirth and music reign around the Hall,
Until the shades of night begin to fall.
Then music ceases, drums no longer sound;
A crowd upon the green lawn gathers round.
The glittering, wondrous works of fire to view,
To many a dalesman's gaze entirely new;
Until a stream of variegated light,
Forms into letters of the words "Good night".
Would it not be far better for the State,
If country gentlemen would imitate
Our generous-hearted friend of Wemmergill?

And to the peasant show as much good-will?
And patronize all manly sports at home,
And not so much in foreign countries roam?
All classes would be more contented soon,
More loyal and devoted to the Crown.
We thank our noble friend with hearts sincere.
Throughout the district all his name revere;
Long may his life be spared to represent
Our interests in the House of Parliament!

The Grove

A SONG

Air—" The Banks of the Dee."

That picturesque country seat "The Grove," the property of H. Surtees, Esq., is situated about two miles north of Woodland Colliery. It stands in a deep valley, on a narrow tongue of land, at the confluence of two mountain brooks— Spolsworth and Shambeny, the former of Black ling Hole celebrity— whose united waters form the Bed Bum, which empties into the Wear in the neighbourhood of Hamsterley. The tall trees and heather-clad hills, which can be seen stretching several miles away to the north and west, have a great charm for lovers of scenery. As a summer sunset picture, it would be difficult to find its superior.

How brightly the red sun sinks down o'er yon mountain,
    Just tinging the west with vermilion and gold,
Reflecting his sheen o'er each clear rill and fountain,
    In streaks of bright sparkling light, fair to behold.
How pleasant to hear the sweet notes of the thrushes
    That sing down the vale where yon mountain brook rushes,
Or watch the wild rabbits among the whin bushes
    That grow in the pastures adjoining The Grove.
I've stood, before now, by fair mansions commanding
    Some fine views of nature, both charming and sweet,
But none like yon structure, so pleasantly standing
    On yonder green point, where two mountain brooks meet
Here Nature's wild beauties are seen to perfection.
They strike the beholder in every direction,
Enhancing the pleasure on closer inspection.
    Enrapturing our souls as we stroll by The Grove.

Let others delight to take up their dwelling
    In cities, where busy scenes meet the eyes sfcill.
To me nature's beauties are far more excelling.
    With sweeter contentment my bosom they fill.

61

No gilding of art to my fancy is wanted,
Give me the lone valley by man seldom haunted,
Where nature's choice gems in profusion are planted
   Adorning this mountain retreat at The Grove.

Perhaps in the future when this frame is laid in
   The cold ground, commingled with its kindred clay.
Some son of the Muses, where now I am treading,
   With self-same emotions the scene may survey.
And as he looks down where yon brooklet is flowing.
As o'er him the Muse her bright mantle is throwing.
His heart with the love of the beautiful glowing.
   May paint in true colours the charms of the Grove.

Old Parkin Raine the Fiddler

A SONG

Ye merry musicians of Teesdale,
   Who love on the fiddle to play,
Who go unto concerts and parties,
   Where music and dancing hold sway;
Your music is sweet, and you please us
   With many a fine melting strain;
But the best of your corps is ta'en from us —
   Our fav'rite, — brave old Parkin Raine!

CHORUS —

   He's gone, "He's gone," and we'll never
      At merry nights see him again;
   But the people of Teesdale will ever
      Remember brave old Parkin Raine!

So neatly the bow he could handle.
   And few men could truer time beat;
We heard his performance with pleasure,
   His tones were so mellow and sweet.
Though praised by the dalesmen around him.
   He ne'er was conceited and vain:
A plain, unassuming, good fellow,
   Was the fiddler — brave old Parkin Raine!

                  Chorus— He's gone, &c.

At fairs, plays, and sports we now miss him,

Where dale lads and lasses oft met
To follow the practice of dancing;
   Those scenes we can never forget.

His polkas, quadrilles, reels, and hornpipes,
   Kept toe and heel going amain;
Few men were so skilled in such music,
   As the fiddler old Parkin Raine!

                    Chorus —He's gone, &c.

When farmers had finished their harvest.
   They often for Parkin did send.
And got all their workers together,
   A jovial evening to spend;
And many a stout country damsel.
   And many a bard handed swain,
Kept up the enjoyment till morning.
   To the music of old Parkin Raine!

                    Chorus — He's gone, (fee.

He always was hearty and cheerful,
   And ne'er in the least thought it wrong
To mingle with social people.
   And sing a good old hunting song.
But the cry of the hounds pleased him better,
   As tbey sped over hill, dale, and plain,
With the loud tally ho of the hunters;
   A sportsman was old Parkin Raine!

                    Chorus — He's gone, &c.

By Stainmore and Brough they well knew him,
   He did at their holly-nights play;
'Tis long since the holly was lighted,
   The custom is now done away.
His fiddling and hunting are over,
   He's gone from this drear world of pain;
But the people of Teesdale will ever
   Remember brave old Parkin Raine!

                    Chorus — He's gone, &c.

Meet Me Molly In The Dell.

SONG.

Air — "Bonny Charlie's now awa."

Meet me, Molly, in the dell,
   In the cooling evening breeze,

When the corncrake's voice is heard
  In the meadows by the Tees.

CHORUS —

Meet me, Molly, in the dell.
  Meet me, Molly, in the dell,
When the corncrake's voice is heard.
  Meet me, Molly, in the dell.

When thy daily work is o'er,
  Come and take a walk with me;
Sweetest hours of my life.
  Are the few I spend with thee!

Chorus — Meet me, Molly, &c.

What although we both are poor —
  What though fortune be unkind —
Love can smooth the path of life,
  Pleasures were for all design'd.

Chorus — Meet me, Molly, &c.

Think not, Molly, grief and care
  Are unto the poor confined;
Wealth has still its load to bear,
  It cannot buy peace of mind.

Chorus — Meet me, Molly, &c.

Molly, thou hast still been true.
  Though good chances thou hast had,
Yet thou did'st them all forsake.
  For a toiling miner lad.

Chorus — Meet me, Molly, &c.

When the sun sinks in the west.
  O'er the height of Mickle Fell,
And to rest the birds retire.
  Meet me, Molly, in the dell.

Chorus — Meet me, Molly, &c.

Tom Bottoms, the Teesdale Hunter

SONG

Air — Perfect Cure.

Below those towering, rugged rocks.
  Which frown from Hoi wick Fell,

64

In an old cabin built of whin,
　　A hunter bold did dwell.
He was a hardy mountaineer,
　　A sportsman of great fame,
Well known throughout the vale of Tees, —
　　Tom Bottoms was his name.

CHORUS.

　But poor old Tom has gone to rest,
　　　His sporting days are o'er;
　His tallyhoing on the hills
　　　We never shall hear more.

Often he went to Cronkley Scars,
　　Hudeshope, and Mickle Fell;
Hillbeck's dense wood, and Pallet Crag,
　　And Balder banks as well,
And rous'd sly Reynard from his lair.
　　And followed on his trail.
In an exciting glorious hunt
　　O'er miles of hill and dale.

　　　　　　　　　　　Chorus — But poor old Tom, &c.

Old Devonshire, his fav'rite dog.
　　Was ever at his call.
And, when he once got on the scent.
　　Bold Reynard's chance was small.
There was true music in that dog.
　　As he sped o'er the ground.
Swift as an arrow from the bow;
　　He was a gallant hound!

　　　　　　　　　　　Chorus — But poor old Tom, &c.

He kept a set of terriers, too;
　　The best in all the North;
The least of them was always fit
　　To draw the badger forth.
And often Tom was heard to say,
　　I'll not depend on man,
Lest I should disappointed be,
　　But on my dogs I can.

　　　　　　　　　　　Chorus — But poor old Tom, &c.

'Twas pleasant, in the months of spring,
　　To wake at early morn,
And hear his voice upon the hills,
　　Strong as a bugle horn!

In capturing the beasts of prey
    No one could him excel;
He was well up to all their tricks,
    And knew their haunts right well.

Chorus — But poor old Tom, &c.

When stormy winter had set in,
    And Boreas loud did roar,
And hunting time was past, oft he
    Was pressed by hunger sore.
Then he would mount his old white mare,
    And roam for many a mile;
Collecting spoil where'er he could.
    In the true gipsy style.

Chorus — But poor old Tom, &c

And when he homeward took his way,
    And had the Tees to cross.
Although the stream was broad and deep,
    He ne'er was at a loss;
He and his mare dash'd boldly in,
    They ne'er were known to fail,
The mare swam over with her load,
    Tom hung on by her tail!

Chorus — But poor old Tom, &c.

One stormy night, by Hudeshope Burn,
    This strange old hunter died!
Poor little Jack stood weeping by,
    His dogs lay by his side.
Thus, 'mid those strange companions, he
    Resign'd his fleeting breath.
And the best voice in Teesdale was
    For ever hushed in death.

Chorus — Now poor old Tom, &c.

Our Friends Beyond The Sea

SONG.

Air — "My Highland Home."

Beneath a spreading tree,
    Close to the river side,
I musing sat, and watched
    The limpid waters glide.
I thought of days of yore.

66

And friends once dear to me.
Who left our lovely vale.
   And are beyond the sea.

CHORUS.

We never can forget,
   Amid our social glee,
Our absent ones from home,
   Our friends beyond the sea.

Childhood's companions, who
   Did often with me play
By yonder pebbly shore,
   Alas! Where now are they?
They're scattered like the Jews,
   But few remain at home;
Some sleep beneath the sod.
   Some o'er the ocean roam.

                     Chorus — We never can forget, &c.

In wild Canadian woods
   Where giant pine trees grow;
In prairies of the West
   Where roams the buffalo;
In India's torrid clime.
   On Afric's sunny ground.
And, on Australian plains,
   Our Teesdale men are found.

                     Chorus — We never can forget, &c.

While sleeping, — they'll behold.
   In many a pleasant dream,
The old familiar walk,
   By rock, and wood, and stream.
But the sweet vision fades
   At the approach of day,
And, with a sigh, they find
   Those scenes are far away.

                     Chorus — We never can forget, &c.

When plenty crowns the board,
   And cheerful tankards foam,
Often the toast will be,
   "The good old folk at home!"
And we, with hearts as warm.
   Shall let our *chief* toast be, —
Our absent ones from home.

Our friends beyond the sea!

Chorus — We never can forget, &c.

Sowing Tares among the Wheat

SONG.

Air — "Castles in the Air."

Of Adam's fallen creatures.
  The meanest in our eyes
Are busy, meddling people.
  Who never stick at lies;
Who, hog-like, thrust their noses
  In other folk's affairs;
And, like their master 'mong the wheat,
  Are *always* sowing tares!
In families making mischief;
  Turning friends to foes;
Rousing evil passions;
  And that without a cause.
Unto the Prince of Darkness
  Such folk are slaves complete;
They do his dirty labour,
  Sowing tares among the wheat.
When an erring neighbour
  Has done an action bad,
Instead of being griev'd thereat,
  Too many will feel glad,
And quickly o'er the country
  They'll tell it o'er with glee;
Only what's vile is brought to light,
  The good they never see!
They'll add unto the story.
  And make it ten times worse, —
Such beings in society
  Are far it's greatest curse.
Should such profess religion,
  'Tis only counterfeit;
No true Christian will be found
  Sowing tares among the wheat

Our Saviour when on earth did give
  A maxim good and sage,

Adapted to all nations,
    Also to every age:
Do unto others as ye would
    That they should do to you;
Those who observe this golden rule
    We know are Christians true.
It is of small importance
    To what sect we belong,
It is the heart, and that alone,
    Which makes us right or wrong.
All men have their failings,
    Yet this we may repeat:
No Christian will be found
    Sowing tares among the wheat

But there's a harvest coming,
    As scriptures plainly say:
The wheat shall all be gathered in.
    And tares be cast away.
And all that's mean and servile,
    From joy shall be debar'd;
The righteous they alone shall gain
    A glorious — good reward.
The living all shall changed be, —
    And graves give up their dead;
Some will be filled with gladness,
    And some with guilty dread.
All nations shall be gathered
    Before the judgment seat;
And then shall cease for ever
    Sowing tares among the wheat

Jack Nicholson

SONG.

Air — "Doran's Ass"

Jack Nicholson a carrier was,
    By Egglesburn he us'd to dwell;
A curious, witty man was he.
    In Teesdale he was known right well
None better loved a glass than he,

And none more fond than he of fun;
The shrewdest men in all the dale
  Could not out-scheme Jack Nicholson.

Taking the lead ore from the mines.
  He went to Blackton every day;
Some smelters there were very rude,
  And a vile trick did on him play.
His dinner they contrived to steal.
  They ate it up and left him none;
Yet never a grumble or complaint
  Was heard from sly Jack Nicholson.

No vegetarian was Jack,
  He lov'd to eat his bread and beef;
"They think they've trick'd me well," said he,
  "But I will soon find out the thief;
They shall not stinted be of meat,
  I'll give them what will spoil their fun —
Something quite easy to digest,
  Or my name's not Jack Nicholson."

Upon the stones by the burn side,
  The carcass of an old horse lay;
Its owner, after skinning it,
  Had plac'd it there out of the way:
Jack, when he saw it, smiled and said,
  "Here's beef for every mother's son;
The greedy smelters at the mill
  Shall learn to know Jack Nicholson."

He cut two pieces from the flank.
  And wrapped them up beside his bread,
And straightway took it to the mill —
  "Now they can eat it up," he said!
The thievish smelters, as before,
  Soon drew it forth when he was gone,
They ate the carrion and the bread.
  And thought they'd trick'd Jack Nicholson.

Jack — when he missed it — laughed and said,
  "To eat my beef you seem inclined.
You're very welcome, it is cheap,
  And more on the bum stones you'll find;

I got it from a carcass there,
    That now lies stinking in the sun;
If you want more you need but speak.
    And I'm your man. Jack Nicholson!"

When this they heard, the guilty men
    Began to groan and vomit sore,
As if their very insides would
    Be vomited upon the floor.
"Ha! ha!" said Jack, "you've got a dose, -
    Somebody for a doctor run, —
Your stomachs cannot stand my beef,
    'Tis far too strong," said Nicholson!

Jack still kept going to the mill,
    Driving his jaggers as before;
The smelters had a lesson learned.
    They never stole his dinner more:
They found out Jack was far too sly.
    And not so easy to be done;
To bite him was but to be bit, —
    What think you of Jack Nicholson?

The Chase

Air—"The Drover Boy"

Of all the gay sports which an Englishman loves.
    The oldest and best is the chase;
Our fathers, we're told, used to follow the hounds.
    And were a bold martial race.
        Our heather clad fells.
        And deep woody dells,
    Did echo to their loud tallyho,
When man, horse, and hound, gaily sped o'er the ground.
    It was pleasant a hunting to go.

Fitzhugh was a soldier, and sportsman as well;
    He oft with his men stout and true,
        Balder, and Lune, and the banks of the Tees,
        Did the wild bounding deer pursue.
            In the early mom,
            The sound of his horn,
        With the cry of a loud tallyho!

71

Caused many a dalesman to rise from his bed,
  And straightway a hunting to go.

From our valleys and hills the wild deer have gone,
  Yet still we've the fox and the hare;
Of pleasures our fathers derived from the sport,
  We may still at this day have our share.
        With our gallant pack,
        We nothing do lack.
    To secure a good run, — tallyho!
When pussy and reynard are vigorous and strong.
    It is pleasant a hunting to go.

Ye, whose occupation requires you to sit
  In your houses nigh every day,
Till your limbs become weak, and the bright hue of health
  From your faces is fading away.
        You'll find 'tis your plan.
        Go and hunt when you can.
    And join in a loud tallyho!
Fresh vigour and strength 'twill impart to your frames.
    If only a hunting you'll go.

Ye nobles of Britain on pleasure intent.
  Ye need not in foreign lands roam;
More loved and respected you're sure all to be
  If you'll join in the gay sports at home
        With your countrymen,
        Over mountain and glen,
    Swell the chorus of loud tallyho!
When gentlemen choose to encourage the sport,
    It is pleasant a hunting to go.

Cronkley Hunt

SONG.

On the ninth of October, one dull misty mom.
We gathered our hounds by the sound of the horn,
And set out from Middleton with hearts beating high,
Resolved all to join in the old hunting cry —
        Tallyho! Tallyho!
        It was all for the sound of a sweet Tallyho!

There were Bellman and Tippler, good dogs we all know;
There were Ringwood, and Ranger, and Gamester also;
And Rover, and Rival, and brave Leader, too;
With Galbert, and Chorus — all hounds good and true.
    Tallyho! &c.

We cross'd o'er the mountain, we made no delay.
And up the Lune Valley we straight took our way.
Till we came to Close House, and, as 'twas our plan,
To range the ground over we quickly began.
    Tallyho! &c.

By the Long Crags the music of Bellman broke forth,
When Reynard broke cover and fled to the north;
To Mickle Fell, swift as an arrow, he flew.
While sportsmen and dogs did most hotly pursue.
    Tallyho! &c.

He ran from the fell-top and westward he fled,
By Coal Syke's moss-water, and round Scordale Head;
Then turning abruptly, a sly trick to play,
Down Maize Beck for Birkdale he then took his way.
    Tallyho! &c.
In spite of his doubling we never went wrong.
Our hounds were all true and the scent was so strong;
We dash'd on with speed o'er the rough craggy ground.
And the hills and the ravines echoed the sound.
    Tallyho! &c.

He cross'd o'er the river by fam'd Falcon Clint,
And in the direction of Harwood he went;
But long o'er the water he did not remain.
For Cronkley he made, and the Tees cross'd again.
    Tallyho! &c.

Bold Reynard, though strong when the chase first begun.
Was getting exhausted, his race was nigh run;
We fast gained upon him as onward he fled,
'Mong the juniper bushes around Hoi wick Head.
    Tallyho! &c.

We gave him no rest, but did quickly pursue.
Old Rover then led when we had him in view,
And we soon overtook him on rough Cronkley Fell,

And cut off his brush when beside the White Well
                    Tallyho! &c.

Success unto Robinson, Raisbeck, and Scott!
Their names, as bold sportsmen, can ne'er be forgot;
And long may our gentry, their sinews to brace.
Encourage and follow the joys of the chase!
                    Tallyho! &c.

O Mary, Will You Go?

Air — Prima Donna Waltz.

O Mary, will you go
    Across the raging seas?
And seek a home in a foreign land.
    And leave the banks of Tees?
And bid farewell to the shady bowers
Where spent we so many happy hours.
And where we gathered the wild flowers, -
    In childhood's early day?
            O Mary, will you go?
            O Mary, will you go
    Across the sea, along with me?
            O Mary, will you go?
O stay, dear Willie, stay! —
    Why leave your home and friends?
And learn to be content with what
    Our heavenly Father sends.
And Willie, don't yourself deceive.
And men's fine gilded tales believe.
Hardships you'll find, your heart to grieve,
    When you are far away.
            O stay, dear Willie, stay!
            O stay, dear Willie, stay!
        Enough you'll find to pain your mind.
            When you are far away.

Mary, what is there here
    But toil and poverty?
As for the friends you're speaking of,
    What have they done for me?
Here I may sweat, and dig for lead,
'Mid smoke and dust, to earn my breads
74

And go half clothed and half fed.
　　Till I can work no more.
　　　　O Mary, will you go? &c.

Dear Willie, in yonder land,
　　Small comfort there is found,
The miners dwell in wretched huts.
　　And sleep on the damp ground.
Besides, dear Willie, bear in mind.
There's rav'nous beasts of every kind.
And poisonous serpents there you'll find
　　Whose bite is instant death.
　　　　O stay, dear Willie, stay, &c.

O Mary, calm your fears,
　　Though rav'nous beasts there are,
Yet rav'nous ones, of human kind.
　　They are the worst by far.
And, Mary dear, to tell you plain,
All your persuasions are in vain;
Next week, I mean to cross the main.
　　So, Mary, will you go?
　　　　O Mary, will you go? &c.
Since, then, to emigrate
　　You seem so much inclined,
I'll just pack up my clothes and go,
　　I will not stay behind.
And, Willie, I'll be thy wedded wife, —
Though cares and troubles should be rife,
I'll cheer and comfort thee through life.
　　　　Dear Willie, I will go.
　　　　O Willie, I will go!
　　　　Dear Willie, I will go!
　　Across the sea, along with thee.
　　　　Dear Willie, I will go!

Past and Present Times

SONG.

Air— "The Old Scotch Bangs for me."

As I was walking out one day
　　Down by the river side,

Beneath a shady, spreading elm
   An aged man I 'spied.
He looked around, and thus he spoke,
   "A question I'll ask thee, —
Are men as happy now-a-days
   As erst they used to be?"

"I'll answer what yon ask," said I,
   "I think men better far;
We've railways and we've telegraphs,
   We more connected are:
Wages are higher, means are more.
   All this is plain to see,
And men are better now-a-days
   Than erst they used to be."

"Although the means are more," paid he,
   "This cannot be denied,
Our wants are still not less but more.
   We've ten times as much pride:
Wages were low, provisions too.
   Were in the same degree;
Men are no better now-a-days
   Than erst they used to be."
"Many a miner of this dale.
   In former times, 'tis said.
Wrought 'mong bad air, and dust, and smoke,
   And lived on black rye bread;
But things have undergone a change.
   As you'll at once agree.
And men are better now-a-days
   Than erst they used to be."

"In bygone times, our fathers brave,
   No finer clothing sought
Than breeches, made of corduroy,
   And the warm home-spun coat;
Ready each other to assist,
   They were both kind and free;
Men are no better now-a-days.
   Than erst they used to be."

"In former times, of which you speak,
   Men wicked tricks could play;

Their dispositions were the same
    As at this present day.
There still has been, since Adam's time.
    The selfish and the free;
And men are better now-a-days
    Than erst they used to be."

"Merit, of old, the standard was.
    But they have changed the plan;
It seems to be the general rule.
    That money makes the man.
To gather it by hook or crook
    Is the chief aim you see;
Men are no better now-a-days
    Than erst they used to be."

"When age and weakness on us creep.
    We think of days of youth;
The recollection oft beguiles.
    We cannot see the truth.
Though light and knowledge still progress,
    As all learned men agree;
And men are better now-a-days
    Than erst they used to be."

All I could say failed to convince
The old man he was wrong,
I saw it would be useless, quite,
The subject to prolong;
He only shook his head and said,
"The good old times give me!
Men are no better now-a-days
Than erst they used to be."

Fairy Dell

SONG.

Air — "When you and I were young."

Come sit you down, dear Nancy,
    By t' fire, while you and I
Converse together, Nancy,
    Of happy days gone by.

We've pretty scenes in Teesdale,
   But none I love so well.
As that sweet place by Millbeck,
   Known as the Fairy DelL

CHORUS.

Nancy, O Nancy,
   I know you remember well.
The happy hours we spent, love,
   Up in the Fairy Dell.
My youthful days, dear Nancy,
   Seem like a pleasant dream,
When arm in arm we rambled
   By the rippling silvery stream.
We gathered nuts and sloes, love.
   And wild flowers you loved well,
By shady bower and rock, love.
   Up in the Fairy Dell.

Chorus — Nancy, O Nancy, &c.

When you were at the town, Nancy,
   I met you oft at night.
Lest bogles of Unthank, Nancy,
   Should put you in a fright;
Your fears fled when I met you.
   As you'll remember well,
We often kissed and promised
   To meet in Fairy Dell.

Chorus — Nancy, O Nancy, &c.

Since then, my dearest Nancy,
   We've in strange places been;
We've wandered far from Teesdale,
   And curious sights we've seen;
Your hair is turning grey, love.
   Yet I love you as well
As when we strolled together,
   Up in the Fairy Dell.

Chorus — Nancy, O Nancy, &c.

We're going down the hill, Nancy,
   Soon at its foot we'll fall,
And youthful days, dear Nancy,
   We never can recall.
I hope we both are going,
   To where bright spirits dwell;
Where we will happier be, love,

Than in the Fairy Dell.

Chorus — Nancy, O Nancy, &c.

Little Bobby Johnson

SONG.

Air — "Perhaps she's on the railway."

Now, if you'll give attention,
   I'll sing a little song,
'Tis of a curious little man.
   As broad as he was long.
They called him Bobby Johnson;
   The farmers knew him well;
And many a funny story.
   They could of Bobby tell.

CHORUS.

   Little Bobby Johnson,
      What a funny chap!
   With his fustian jacket
      And his old brown hairy cap.
Waddling along, sirs, on the dusty road;
Like a tinker's donkey, beneath a heavy load.

He was a famed mechanic,
   One of the very best;
The clocks that kept the truest time,
   Were just the ones he dress'd.
With stock of all description,
   A skilful man was he
When he was in the humour,
   And the witches let him be!

Chorus — Little Bobby Johnson, &c.

He'd forty pockets in his coat.
   In which he kept his tools;
He'd hammers, pincers, compasses.
   Nails, knives, and measuring rules,
And bits of leather, wax, and ends.
   Bolts, screws, and bull snout rings;
With tin and wooden boxes too,
   And various other things.

Chorus — Little Bobby Johnson, &c.

79

Such food as puddings, beef, or pies,
   He did not care to see;
His fav'rite dish, where'er he went.
   Was tough pancake and tea!
He used no milk or sugar.
   But always salt instead!
And when he saw an onion,
   Away in haste he fled!

                                      Chorus— Little Bobby Johnson, &c.

Of fairies, ghosts, and witches,
   He always was in dread!
They got into his chamber.
   And teased him in his bed!
They pulled the blankets off him,
   And played him many a trick;
And brought a smell of onions.
   Which made poor Bobby sick!

                                      Chorus — Little Bobby Johnson, &c.

He burnt hen hearts to keep them out,
   But 'twas of no avail.
In spite of all his spells and charms
   They did him still assail
But Bobby ne'er loved women,
   He did them always slight;
And when the witches stirred him up
   They only served him right.

                                      Chorus — Little Bobby Johnson, &c.

Now all men have their weakness,
   As you'll at once agree;
The wisest men, you'll find, are not
   From superstition free.
Mere trifles will annoy us.
   And often trouble bring —
Although not hags or onions —
   Some other foolish thing.

                                      Chorus — Little Bobby Johnson, &c.

Old Gowling

A well-known jack of all trades, and a noted performer on the cymbals.

SONG.

Air— "Marble Arch."

There dwelt a man at our town end,
   Whom few could understand,
He often disappointed was
   With ought he took in hand.
Old Gowling was the name he bore,
   When ought disturbed his breast.
He had a curious way indeed
   To set his mind at rest.

CHORUS.

   He took his cymbals down
      His sorrows to allay.
   With tinkling and jingling
      To drive dull care away.

As he could write and make up sums,
   To keep a school he tried;
And though he used both rod and strap,
   The boys he could not guide.
They burnt his switch, and spilt his ink,
   And placed pins in his chair,
Which wounded him when he sat down.
   And made him curse and swear.

Chorus — He took his cymbals, &c.

Disgusted, he gave up the school,
   Candles to make began,
Both wick and tallow he procured,
   Also a. melting pan.
One day into the pan he fell,
   Among the scalding fat,
Which made him roar with pain, and say,
   "I'll have no more of that!"

Chorus — He took his cymbals, &c.

He next a gardener became;
   Greens and gooseberries sold.

With apples, cherries, pears, and plums,
   Potatoes too I'm told.
But grubs and caterpillars vile
   Vex'd him in such a way,
He had to give up gardening;
   He said it would not pay.

                       Chorus —He took his cymbals, &c.

He next was bellman of our town;
   His voice was strong and clear.
And, to add to his means, he soon
   Became an auctioneer.
And in this line of business,
   No bad attempt he made.
But he could not a living gain,
   There was so little trade.

                       Chorus— He took his cymbals, &c.

Soon, with a pretty buxom lass
   He deeply fell in love,
She married him just for his brass,
   And did unfaithful prove.
They kept a beer shop awhile.
   Things went wrong every day;
He was well fleeced and jilted too,
   His Phoebe ran away.

                  Chorus — Yet he took his cymbals, &c

The beer shop he soon gave up.
   He'd formed another plan,
It was a showman to become,
   And have a caravan.
Fine pictures he from London got,
   With everything first rate;
Alas! poor man, it would not do —
   Expenses were so great.

                Chorus — Then he took his cymbals, &c.
To make his show still more complete.
   He did a monkey get.
Intending, though an ugly brute.
   To keep it for a pet;
But to his sorrow, he soon found.
   That he a pest had got —
Dabbling its nasty hairy paws
   Into his treacle pot.

                Chorus — Then he took his cymbals, &c.

To make it less mischievous,

He gave it oft its licks;
But his severe correction failed
  To cure it of its tricks.
His broken pots and glasses too
  Did fill his heart with woe,
He, in a fit of passion, sold
  Both monkey and the show.

Chorus — Then he took his cymbals, &c.

To tell the numerous trades he tried
  I know would tedious be.
The best of schemes will go awry.
  As you'll at once agree.
And he has done with all his plans,
  He's on another shore.
Where earthly cares no more annoy.
  And where he never more

Chorus — Shall take his cymbals, &c.

Now from this simple home-spun song
  We may a lesson learn;
The reason why he often failed
  You may at once discern.
Had perseverance been combined
  With talent he possessed.
The cymbals he need not have ta'en
  To set his mind at rest

Chorus — Nor took his cymbals, &c.

What Will My Mother Say?

SONG.

Air — "Kiss me quick and go,"

As I was walking out one day.
  In the sweet month of June,
I met a pretty country girl,
  Returning from the town;
"You're laden hard, my dear," said I,
  "I'll set you on your way."
"Oh no," said she, "it must not be, —
  What will my mother say?"

"My dear, your mother once was young,
 And loved, and courted too;
'Tis easy for old folk to say
 What young ones ought to do."
"This may be true," said she "but yet
 Young girls are led astray;
And often rue they did not mind.
 What mother had to say."

"My mother brought me up, and did
 My childish footsteps guide
I was a baby at her breast.
 When my dear father died.
Although you may my fancy please,
 Yet I will not give way
Unto my fancy, till I know
 What mother had to say."

Said I "You're just the girl for me!
 I care for none but you;
A girl who minds her parent's wish,
 Will mind a husband's too.
'Tis best to marry when we're young;
 Therefore I'll not delay,
But go with you at once and hear
 What mother has to say."

Now seven years we've married been,
 A happy pair are we!
Three lovely children I have got,
 To climb upon my knee.
I often smile and say to them.
 As with their toys they play,
"Hush! children, do not make a noise.
 What will your mother say?"

Black Ling Hole

SONG.

The day is waning fast, my dear.
The evening's cool, the sky is clear,
Bright Phoebus soon will disappear.
 And night's dark shadows fall;

Come, my lassie, let us away.
And in yonder valley stray.
And view the scenes of nature gay
    Down in the Black Ling Hole.

A pretty place is the Black Ling Hole,
Where Bedburn's limpid waters roll.
The sparkling pool and the waterfall,
    These are the scenes for me.

Young Nellie on a ramble bent,
Along with me she blythely went,
A pleasant hour or two we spent
    Beneath the larches tall;
Sweet flowers perfumed the evening breeze.
The birds sang sweetly on the trees.
And everything conspired to please,
    Down by the Black ling Hole.

Chorus— A pretty, &c.

But birds and trees and flowers fair
Could not with Nellie's self compare;
She was the loveliest flower there,
    And pleased me best of all;
I threw my arms around her waist
While I to her my love confessed.
And kisses on her lips I pressed
    Down by the Black Ling Hole.

Chorus — A pretty, &c.

"Hold on, be not too bold," said she,
"Or else I fear we'll disagree.
And then I'll come no more with thee
    Out on an evening stroll;
Thy love in proper bounds confine.
Till thou canst fairly call me thine,
Nor let me think an ill design
    Brought thee to Black Ling Hole."

Chorus — A pretty, &c.

"My dear," said I, "you may believe
I am not of those who would deceive,
Nor would I cause thy heart to grieve
    Even in matters small.
If you'll consent my bride to be,
A loving heart you'll find in me,

85

And you will never rue that we
   Met at the Black Ling Hole.

Chorus — A pretty, &c.

The question popped, she gave consent;
Soon after to the church we went.
We married were, and live content
   Although our means are small.
Oft on a pleasant summer day
Across the fields we take our way,
And view the scenes of nature gay,
   Down in the Black Ling Hole.

Chorus — A pretty, &c.

Teesdale Rifle Volunteers

SONG.

Air — "Come under my 'plaidie."

You lovers of scenery, majestic and grand,
You've no need to wander in a foreign land;
Here nothing is wanting your fancy to please,
Few places you'll find like the Vale of the Tees.
Our young men are sprightly, our damsels are pretty,
Yet unto observers this plainly appears;
Take farmers, mechanics, clerks, tradesmen and miners,
The pick of our men are our brave volunteers.
By clear mountain rill, and by heather-clad fell.
By steep rugged rock, and by flowery dell,
By cat'ract and fountain, by wood and green lea.
Where Tees rolls along in its course to the sea,
Dwell hearts stout and loyal as any in Britain,
Unshrinking and fearless when danger appears;
Enduring and steady, at duty's call ready,
And these are the men to make brave Volunteers.

The trophies they've won testify of their skill;
What corps in the north more efficient in drill?
It gives the whole dale satisfaction to know,
Their mark they still make wheresoever they go.
Long may they continue and keep up their honour,
Because every dalesman is proud when he hears
Venerated by strangers away from our valley,
Great feats of skill done by our brave Volunteers.

Britannia securely may rest at her ease,
With brave men on shore and brave tars on the seas;
Nor will her bright laurels e'er droop in decay,
While justice and truth are upheld on her way.'
Though foes league against her, and bluster and threaten,
Not all their whole forces united she fears;
They may speak of invasion, but dare not attempt it.
They guess well the pluck of our brave volunteers.

Long life to your leaders! the country well knows
The zeal they have always displayed in the cause.
Likewise to subordinate officers too.
Who have to their duty been faithful and true.
May hearts stout and loyal be never found wanting.
When this generation from earth disappears,
Young men who will follow the steps of their fathers.
And stand in the ranks of our brave Volunteers.

Lovely Sweet Vale of the Tees

SONG.

Air— "Beautiful Isle of the Sea"

Lovely sweet vale of the Tees!
    Still thou art dear as ever.
Thy rocks, dells, and shady green trees.
    Thy meadows and murmuring river,
Valley where happiest hours
    Of childhood were joyously squandered.
As by thy meandering stream.
    Thy rare beauties viewing I wandered.

CHORUS.

No matter what be my lot,
    Thy beauties shall ne'er fail to please,
A thousand ties bind me to thee,
    Lovely sweet vale of the Tees!

Here's Cauldron Snout and High Force,
    Magnificent sights worth surveying.
Wherever our footsteps may turn
    New scenes are their beauties displaying,

And rare ferns and flowers adorn
   Thy rocks, dells, and shady green bowers;
Thy sons are enduring and bold,
   Thy daughters are fair as thy flowers.

Chorus — No matter, &c.

Down further stands Baliol's Tower,
   Where Teesdale men bravely contended
'Gainst forces fierce, numerous, and strong,
   And nobly their country defended.
Close by Walter Scott mused and wrote
   While feelings of rapture came o'er him.
Which rose from his mind to his pen
   As he viewed the bright landscape before him.

Chorus — No matter, &c.

Sweet vale, though we sing in thy praise.
   Yet life has it's stem earnest duties;
Thy sons in all countries are found.
   Poor men cannot live by thy beauties.
No matter in what clime they dwell,
   Their hearts still retain a warm feeling
To all that reminds them of thee,
   The love of their birthplace revealing.

Chorus— No matter, &c.

My Journey to Work

'Tis Monday morning and Apollo bright
Gilds the far eastern hills with golden light;
To hail the rising orb of day, I hear
The cheerful rousing voice of chanticleer;
From the whin cliffs the wild rock pigeons fly,
And starlings there keep up a chattering cry.
All animated things seem blythe and gay.
Pleased with the prospect of a pleasant day.
With my week's wallet o'er my shoulder flung,
Down the green sloping meads I jog along
A well known path from Holwick to Bowlees,
Where Winch Bridge spans the verdant banks of Tees.
When to the roaring river drawing near,
Its rumbling sound strikes loudly on the ear, —
Foaming and dashing in its rapid course,
O'er the rough grey whin rock named Little Force,
Then flowing gently doth its way pursue,
Till by the Staple Crag 'tis hid from view.

The sun, with no dark cloud to intervene,
Shines brightly on a varied lovely scene;
The tall fir trees that on the north bank grow.
Their shadows long across the river throw,
Forming a picture strange of light and shade,
Where interesting objects are displayed,
To meditate on these I must not stay,
So o'er the creaking chain-bridge take my way.
And through a dense plantation move along,
The ears regaled with many a pleasing song
Of happy birds that flit from tree to tree
And seem, unlike our race, from sadness free.
But, soon emerging from the shady trees.
And, leaving the small village of Bowlees
On my left hand, the dewy footpath leads
Down by Bank Farm and through the flowery meads.
Where cowslip, primrose, clover and heartsease,
With fragrance sweet perfume the morning breeze.
Crossing a brook upon a rough hewn plank.
And going up a short, steep, stony bank,
Newbiggin's reached, where miners often stop
To light their pipes at Willie Gibson's shop.
A blacksmith Willie is, of well-tried skill.
Whom we find hard at work call when we will;
Though toiling hard, he does no strong drink use,
Give him the proffer he'll at once refuse.
He means a staunch teetotaller to remain —
Never to taste the tempting draught again.
Because he's felt its power and therefore tries
To watch, with care, the point where danger lies.
Whene'er we meet he greets me with a smile,
Enquires the news, and bids me rest awhile.
Which I oft do, loving his chat to hear.
Because 'tis from all coarse expressions clear.
Though in our views we sometimes disagree,
It matters not, good humoured still is he.
But here too long the time must not be spent,
Before lies a rough, steep, and long ascent:
Bidding good-bye, and shouldering my load,
I, like a cadger, take again the road,
And through long strips of fenc'd allotments pass.
Where sheep and cattle crop the tender grass.
When past the grounds of Stable Edge, I find
The verdant trees and fields are left behind;

The ground does here a sterile aspect show,
Where bent, coarse grass and stunted heather grow;
From which the merry lark rejoicing springs.
And in the clouds his song of rapture sings.
In circles round me noisy lapwings fly.
While uttering their peculiar cry.
The rugged up-hill walk, and sun's hot rays,
Cause the warm sweat to trickle down the face,
Yet pushing on, the path an ascent still,
Till on the top of bleak Hardberry Hill,
Where sitting down, my wearied limbs to ease,
I, looking back, survey the Vale of Tees.
What a majestic scene can be discerned
When to the far off west the eye is turn'd;
Grim mountain peaks in Alpine grandeur rise,
Which in the distance seem to kiss the skies.
First in the range, from hoary mist not clear;
The outlines dim of high Cross Fell appear.
With Dun Fell, Little Fell, and Meldon too,
And nearer Mickle Fell's broad rocky brow.
A bright scene meets the eye down the vale, where
Neat whitewashed cots stand scattered here and there,
Each with its farm, reclaimed from the wild moor,
Affording comforts to the labouring poor.
No healthier dwellings in our isle are found,
Than those upon the Duke of Cleveland's ground;
Plainly are seen the rugged Cronkley rocks,
Frequented by the prowling, cunning fox.
Because its numerous lengthy caverns yield
Places for shelter, and from foes a shield.
Well may be marked the river's winding course,
Through Cauldron Snout and, nearer, the High Force;
And other interesting objects too.
Behind the hill lie hidden from the view.
Seen are the cliffs in front of Hoi wick Fell,
Also the deep ravine named Fairy Dell;
And Unthank bank, where once a village stood:
The craggy steeps beyond, and Park End wood.
Like a huge serpent, down the dale, is seen
The Tees, all glistening like silver sheen.
Oft curving round some hill, 'tis hidden quite,
Anon appearing in the broad sun light.
And such is life, our brightest visions fade,
Sometimes 'tis bright, anon we're in the shade;

At times we smoothly glide, at others grope
Our gloomy way, with nothing left but hope.
At yon vale foot, where Hudeshope's waters run.
Stands the small market town of Middleton,
Supported by the mines producing lead.
Where many a dalesman labours for his bread;
While others, with. employment are supplied
In the whin quarries on the Yorkshire side.
Northward appears that broad and mighty swell
Of brown moor pasture land, named Arthur Fell,
And Kirk Cairn's little round plantation green,
Which almost from the ocean may be seen;
And further down, more interesting still.
The little ancient church upon the hill.
Next Mickleton appears, distinct to sight.
Beyond where moss-tinged Lune and Tees unite,
With its long street, extending east and west,
And fertile fields, in verdant beauty drest.
My face from Yorkshire for a while I'll turn,
And view that lovely scene past Egglesburn;
'A vapour dense ascends on yonder hill
From the large smelting works of Blackton mill;
Long may it rise in curling wreaths on high,
And ore be raised, each furnace to supply,
To give employment to the neighbouring poor.
And keep the wolf named Want far from their door.
Below, where Neimer's thick-set forest wide.
Eastward extends along yon mountain side.
Lies Eggleston, a village neat and clean,
Though from this mountain indistinctly seen.
The mansion where the worthy squire resides.
Yon intervening hill completely hides.
Straight opposite across the rolling Tees,
Old Romaldkirk lies nestling 'mong the trees.
Its grey church steeple like a giant tall.
With its square form appears above them ail.
Although the village snug meets not my gaze,
Yet well am I acquainted with the place;
Many a happy eve I've in it spent.
In youthful days, when I a-courting went!
'Twas pleasant in the summer time to stray,
And nature's scenes by Lowgarth Farm survey,
Or the green path by Wooden Croft pursue.
And, by the stream, the Fairy Cupboards view.

But here my muse her backward flight must stay,
Lest from my text she draw my mind away
On bygone days to meditate and dream.
When present things must be my only theme.
Now, further down the woody vale I look,
Where Tees is fed by Haider's rippling brook.
Southward, across from Shiply's shaggy wood.
Where gallant Fitzhugh's ancient castle stood,
lies pretty Cotherstone, a healthful place.
Frequented much in the warm summer days
By gentry from our smoky towns, to share
The bracing influence of country air.
The vision now grows cloudy and unclear;
By Lartington more dense the trees appear;
That charming village under Witham's care.
With its neat cots and flower gardens rare.
Though distance dims the view, yet further down
Is seen the smoke of Barnard Castle town;
"Old Barny," — Teesdale's pride and strength of yore.
Which no small share in feudal conflicts bore.
Set 'mid a landscape beautiful and grand.
Adorned by glowing nature's lavish hand.
But not for charming scenery alone
Is this metropolis of Teesdale known.
When England's flag of war has been unfurled,
No matter in what quarter of the world,
Men of this loyal town were never slow
In going forth to battle with the foe.
With gallant Moore, and Wellington in Spain,
On Waterloo's famed sanguinary plain,
Where British pluck was to the utmost tried,
They nobly fought their way, or nobly died.
Those who returned served only to inspire
The rest with the same patriotic fire.
It too, has had its literary men
Of no mean order, wielding well the pen.
And not a few has still, whom I know well.
Though unpretentious, yet do they excel.
In vain I look among yon misty steam
To view that structure grand the Bowes Museum,
Where works of art from distant lands are brought,
By the most famed and skilful artists wrought,
A building which, when finished, cannot fail
To form the chief attraction of our dale.

lovely native vale with fond regard
I look on thee; though dreary, rough, and hard
My way has been, yet no amount of ill
Can loose the ties that bind me to thee still.

* * * * *

Again I take the wallet on my back,
And northward follow on the miner's track;
Unto the sight soon Hudeshope Vale appears.
With the rough broken ground around the Skears,
Broken by bushes, strong in days of yore,
To bare the veins, and to discover ore.
Between those ravines deep are pastures green.
Beyond the summit of the Monks is seen;
While fir plantation patches beautify
Places where heaps of ancient rubbish lie.
Across the mountain ridge my way I wend,
And with brisk step into the vale descend.
On my left hand, Coldberry Mine appears;
The din of mills and jiggers strike the ears;
This sound does from the washing floors proceed,
Where from the dross the mineral is freed.
Those interested in the dressing line
Should pay a visit to this busy mine;
Three chief points gained a skilled observer sees,
These are despatch, economy, and ease.
At Elfatory Foot flows the small brook.
Which, having crossed, my face is turned to look
Upon the muddy waters as they glide
Down past the place where poor old Bottoms died;
Of his lone dwelling there is little trace,
Strong floods have almost swept away the place.
Poor Tom! No more we'll hear his hunting horn
Awake the slumbering echoes of the mom;
Time will not linger j leaving the brown burn.
Unto Lodge Syke old mine ray face I turn.
By far the richest mine in Teesdale seen.
In fact, few in our isle have richer been;
Like ancient Carthage, it has had its run,
'Tis now wrought out, its mineral wealth is done.
Large rubbish heaps along the hill side show
The vast extent of hollow ground below.
Here toiled my father for his bairns' support,
Till poverty and toil his days cut short;
While I was but a boy of tender years.

Unconscious of his cares, his griefs, and fears,
Which like a galling burden he'd to bear,
A legacy of which I've been his heir.
Now silence reigns where clamour reign'd before,
The rattling of machinery is o'er,
The anvil's ringing sound, also the noise
Of labouring men and busy washer boys;
One man alone remains extracting ore
From refuse heaps, of little worth before.
The lodging shops, where miners nightly stayed,
Are into airy cottage dwellings made.
Each with its garden plot, the peaty soil
Repaying well the cotter for his toil.
Now past the verdant patch from rubbish freed.
Where MacNomara's goat and donkey feed;
More wild and dreary grows the aspect round.
Bent and brown heather clothe the mossy ground.
Which give to nature's face a darker hue,
Home of the grouse, the plover, and curlew.
Reaching the summit of the barren hill,
'Tis a rough long descent to Manorgill;
From here is seen, far as sight can extend,
A desert vast, of which there seems no end.
One place alone, like an oasis bright,
Adds variation to the gloomy sight;
It is the well-known farm of Middle End,
Near where two muddy brooks their waters blend.
Crossing the stream, and climbing up steep hill.
Keeping the path to west of Wiregill,
Where a rich prosperous mine is, which employs
A number large of men and washer boys.
The hill top gained, pleased I look round,
Knowing I've done with all the climbing ground.
Before bleak Shaftwell's dark brown hills appear,
Which form the boundary line 'twixt Tees and Wear,
And the squire's shooting box upon the hill.
Which fort-like frowns on Thornberry Gill;
And on a line extending o'er yon ridge,
The long abandoned works of old Flake Bridge.
Passing two reservoirs, built to supply
The works with water when the weather's dry,
And going down an easy gentle slope,
I reach the Rake of Little Eggleshope.
And to the shop beside the mill proceed,

Where from their load my shoulders soon are freed.
After a meal and a short rest, I find
Myself refreshed, and more for work inclined;
Then down the stony burn my footsteps wend,
And reach my cabin at my journey's end.
And now, my muse, begone, go take thy rest.
Thy inspiration suits my leisure best;
I must not be by thy vain fancies led,
'Tis here, and not by thee, I win my bread.

Song

Air — "Fine Old English Gentleman."

Sung at a private party given by a. Metcalfe-Gibson, Esq., to the choir and church-people of the parish of Ravenstonedale, March 7th, 1884.

Ye cheerful guests attention give, now while I strike my lyre,
In praise of a brave gentleman, whom all love and admire,
Whose spirit seems, in generous deeds, to neither lag nor tire,
Possessing all the qualities which Englishmen require
     In a fine old English Gentlemen, one of the olden time.

From Oddendale, in Westmorland, sprang the illustrious line
Of Gibson, a respected name, in after years to shine,
As if it had intended been by Providence divine
To choose such men to carry out some glorious design.
     Through those fine old English, &c.

The Metcalfes, too, our annals show, were a bold martial race.
To Nappa Hall, in Wensleydale, their origin we trace.
Between those noble families an union took place.
Of which has sprung this present branch, our native land to grace
     With fine old English, &c.
The present head of this famed house, by whom we're gathered here.
As one of Britain's noblest sons is noted far and near;
The wealthy justly honour him, the poor his name revere.
Ask all who know him, what he is — they'll answer with a cheer,
     He's a fine old English, &c.

A sportsman keen, from early youth, he's always been inclined
All out-door sports to patronise, when of a manly kind,
But all those of a vicious sort, that tend to lower the mind.
Meet no encouragement from him, low aims he casts behind,

Like a fine old English, &c.

How 'neath his quick unerring aim the becking red grouse fell.
At Black-moss and on Little Fell, his sporting records tell;
And in the keen exciting coarse, brave Barrier and Belle,
With Hughie Grahame, three famed greyhounds, such as none could excel,
    Of this fine old English, &c.

For years, with zeal untiring, 'tis well known he hath sought
The agricultural interests of this country to promote;
His skill in judging short-horned stock, by long experience bought.
Has been approved, and still will be, as Royal Shows denote.
    O this fine old English, &c.

A patriotic soul has he, and feels inclined to be
On the side of good government, order and harmony;
Of the stout Yeoman Cavalry a member long was he.
Because he wished to guard our homes and keep Britannia free.
    Like a fine old English, &c.

The choir and churchmen of this dale for years will not forget
The bounty of their friend, by whom they annually are met,
A noble custom of his house, which will be kept up yet,
At least till life's refulgent sun in radiance shall set
    On this fine old English, &c.

May a kind gracious Providence his useful life long spare,
For such cement the gaps of States and keep it in repair;
And when the closing scene arrives may not a cloud of care
Arise to shade his entrance to the heavenly mansions fair,
    For such a fine old English, &c.

Now may the sons and daughter of this noble parent prove
Worthy their sire, and all weak aims still keep themselves above,
Then shall the hall and cottage vie in loyalty and love,
And form a barrier of defence no adverse power can move,
    By some fine old English, &c.

Britannia's power cannot wane, strong yet shall be her hand.
As long as such brave generous hearts are scattered o'er the land;
Among the nations of the earth due honour they command.
They are our strength, and cause our race first on fame's scroll to stand.
    Do our fine old English, &c.

The Old Oak Tree

A Sketch of the History of Barnard Castle

RECITATIVE.

On a dark, dull, September afternoon,
I took a stroll from Barnard Castle town,
To spend a leisure hour, and view the skill
Of our brave volunteers, up Deepdale Gill;
The murky clouds, which bad been gathering round,
Broke as I reached their shooting practice ground;
I stood beneath an aged oak, to gain
Protection from the heavy pelting rain.
A curious tree, which overhung a rill
Drawn from the brook to drive a busy mill;
Its brown, rough, knotty trunk, in part decayed.
The scathing marks of Time's rough hand displayed;
Yet, though of ancient strength and bloom bereft,
Its green leaves showed some youthful vigour left
While I stood its crook'd figure scanning o'er,
My mind reverting to the days of yore, —
To my surprise, a voice, distinct and clear,
Although not loud, struck strangely on my ear;
I soon found out it issued from the oak,
Which a brief history, like the following, spoke: —

THE OAK.

You seem interested in my time-worn form,
That has withstood for centuries many a storm,
Though I am wearing down, yet none can say
My weakness springs from premature decay.
'Tis now six hundred years, or thereabout.
Since by this limpid brook I first took root.
Sprung from a stock, the pride of British trees,
Upholding England's glory on the seas.
Great changes have indeed ta'en place since then,
In nature's face and in the ways of men;
Westward, extending up the vale of Tees,
Was a dense forest of rough, hardy trees,
Long set apart as royal hunting ground,
Where wild deer roam'd, and food and shelter found.
Oft have I heard the merry hunting horn
Sound sweetly on the chilly breeze of mom,
When noble knights, a gallant sporting race,

Met to enjoy the pleasures of the chase;
And oft this glen has echoed to the sound
Of huntsman's loud shrill voice, and crying hound,
As hotly they pursued the flying stag,
O'er tangling bush, brake, stream, and slippery crag;
Scorning all dangers that lay in their way.
Onward they sped, nought could their ardour stay.
Your modem hunts, pursuing fox or hare.
Can never with the ancient sport compare;
Not the same martial dash do they unfold,
More dull and tame than what they were of old;
Not in the keen exciting chase alone,
Were Teesdale's sons in former ages known;
Well skilled in feats of arms, by fear unmoved.
Their power and native daring oft were proved
In many a hard contested bloody field.
Where both contending parties scorned to yield.
I knew yon Castle in its strength and pride,
When its strong walls our country's foes defied,
A check to each marauding Scottish band.
Who came to spoil and devastate the land.
Oft they have tried, in numbers strong, to gain
Possession of this fortress, but in vain;
The gallant hearts with whom they had to deal,
With steady aim, soon caused their ranks to reel.
Thus the invaders, foiled in their desire.
With heavy loss, compelled were to retire.
So failed the forces Scotland's monarch led,
Who were in yon green sloping pastures spread,
And there Eustace de Vescey I saw fall,
Struck by a missile from the Castle wall;
And as they gently raised him from the ground,
"A bolt," said they, "hath dealt this ghastly wound."
Their King beheld, with feelings of deep grief.
The gory form of the expiring chief —
"Be what it may which has done this," said he,
"I feel a dear bolt it has been to me!"
Yon pasture ground, the scene of that affray,
Retains the name of "Dear Bolt" to this day.
Not much above a sapling I had grown
When the third Richard sat upon the throne,
A King unfortunate, whom writers place
In no high standing 'mong our royal race.
Ascribing to him base dark deeds of blood.

Yet showing no just reason why they should.
Too much the thoughtless way 'tis with mankind,
Without investigation faults to find.
And paint dark things with a still darker hue.
Keeping the good and beautiful from view.
No matter what vain scribblers set him down.
At least he was a true friend to this town:
To keep its martial strength up, he took care
The weak points of the Castle to repair.
He planned a church and college, too, and sought
The valley's real welfare to promote;
And more he might have done, had not his foes
Brought his career to an untimely close.
Poor Monarch! crown and life he had to yield
On Bosworth's hard-fought sanguinary field.
His name we'll still respect for what we know;
What is not clearly proven let it go.
When disaffected nobles of the north,
To war sent their armed rebel legions forth,
Trusting in their united strength, they swore
By force they would the ancient faith restore,
And have one of their choice and creed to reign,
And their lost power and influence regain.
With gathering strength the plot spread o'er the land.
The rising flame by stubborn bigots fanned.
A mid this scene of civil strife and blood
True to their sovereign Barnard's warriors stood,
And raised the royal standard on the wall,
By it resolved to bravely stand or fall.
The gallant Sir George Bowes, of knightly fame,
To be their chief from Streatlam Castle came,
Although his soldiers were in number few.
Their loyalty and courage well he knew.
They hailed his coming with a ringing cheer.
With such a leader bold they felt no fear.
Need for their skill and courage they soon found,
When the strong rebel host came on the ground;
Rank after rank, like an advancing tide.
Closing the castle round on every side,
Bidding the garrison to yield or die,
Shouts of defiance they got for reply.
Enraged at this they did their squadrons form,
And fix their guns to take the place by storm;
As ocean waves dash 'gainst a rocky shore

With fearful force, when stormy tempests roar,
So rushed the rebels on to the attack.
But only to be foiled and driven back
Before the deadly fire poured from within,
Their ardour slackened, and their ranks grew thin.
No easy task had the defenders stout
To keep the obstinate invaders out.
Hard pressed, hemmed in, assailed on every side,
Pluck and endurance were severely tried;
Yet not one failed, all nobly fought and well,
Each stepping forward where a comrade fell.
Sir George, their leader, flew from post to post,
Guarding with care where danger threatened most.
Cheering his men, inspiring in each breast
The selfsame feelings he himself possessed.
Thus, amid fire, smoke, dust and falling stones.
The sounds of warfare and of dying groans.
They struggled night by night and day by day,
Keeping the desperate enemy at bay;
But want of water was their greatest foe.
Thirst crushed their hopes and brought them low,
And for their enemies the Castle won.
Which they by force of arms could not have done.
But not dishonoured or yet put to rout.
With waving flags and music they marched out.
Knowing a force was near too strong to meet,
Barnard's invaders soon beat a retreat.
Since then this lovely vale has had no cause
Of fear or trouble from invading foes.
In these late years of civil peace and rest,
Science and art have rapidly progress'd.
Large factories have been built and railroads made
For the requirements of increasing trade.
Few nobler structures have we in the land
Than yonder Mansion, beautiful and grand,
Which tends so greatly to adorn this town
And add to its attraction and renown,
Built by a Bowes, of the same line and blood
As he who boldly 'gainst the rebels stood.
Who did this place to rear a mansion choose
In memory of his late lamented spouse.
Countess Montalbo, a lady well beloved,
Whose acts benevolent her goodness proved.
Long may her husband yet be spared to find

True pleasure in the work he has designed.
Possessing still the same untiring zeal
His ancestors had for their country's weal.
And keep unsullied the undying fame
Attached to his illustrious race and name.
Speaking again of dalesmen, not alone
In civil contests was their power shown;
In all our struggles hard with foreign foes
They bore their part true to their country's cause.
Well I remember first Napoleon's days,
How he contrived large armaments to raise,
And pushed his eagles on till Europe lay
Panting, exhausted, crushed beneath his sway,
Except our little Isle, that scorned his yoke.
And firmly stood when other nations broke.
Till Waterloo was fought, and "Bonny" found
His army crushed, his hopes dashed to the ground.
Many a gallant regiment I have known.
On finer looking men sun never shone,
Leave this small town each with a lightsome heart,
In the stern work of death to take their part;
And as they gaily marched along the street,
Music swelled on the air, and drums were beat,
As if they had been blythely going forth
To some gay festal scene of joy and mirth.
They left, their country's glory to maintain:
Alas! how few saw Teesdale's hills again!
In Portugal and Spain, in Egypt, too.
And in the gory field of Waterloo
Their ashes lie, and doubtless will remain
Till the last trump cause earth to yield her slain.
Well pleased am I, although I'm but a tree,
A gathering such as at this day to see,
When dalesmen meet with feelings of good will
In this romantic glen to try their skill,
And the same martial bearing to behold
As what was in their ancestors of old.
No doubt have I that they would boldly show
A dangerous front to an invading foe.
And fail in nought that duty's call requires,
But prove true Britons worthy of their sires.
Of England's future standing I've no fears,
While she has her brave Rifle Volunteers;
And 'tis her wisest policy, I'm sure,

To keep up her vast military power;
Nor through vain saving thoughts let it decrease;
To be well set for war secures us peace.
Long may peace reign and useful arts advance.
The comfort of all classes to enhance,
And in the front may Teesdale take its place
In all that dignifies the human race.
And now a brief sketch of my life thou'st got,
No doubt thou wilt suppose I know thee not:
I knew thee from the first, and what I've said
Will shortly in the Mercury be read.
Well, be it so, in writing do not slack,
Though mushroom friends should on thee turn their back;
Nor let thy poverty be an excuse
For thee to cast aside or slight the Muse.
Be not discouraged or in mind cast down,
Nor hang thy head though fickle fortune frown;
Bear this in mind, thou standest not alone,
Many for bread ere now have got a stone:
Still sing thy local songs and tell thy tales,
And when thy voice and musing power fails.
Go to that rest which for the good remains,
And unto others leave thy pleasing strains.
May the All-wise Director prosper thee,
So wishes thy true friend, the Old Oak Tree.

    It ceased to speak, the sky grew clear,
        I left the little brook;
    And to the town, across the bridge,
        My way I quickly took.

www.ingramcontent.com/pod-product-compliance
Lightning Source LLC
Chambersburg PA
CBHW051843040426
42447CB00006B/669